"The psalmist's question 'How shall we : continues to haunt many Christians tod. the answers given vary widely. Where, then, is wisdom to be found? In *Empowered Witness*, Alan Strange offers us a much-needed combination of historical learning, biblical thinking, and deep love for the church. Rather than browbeat us into sharing prejudices, *Empowered Witness* serves us by helping us think. In expressing the 'reasonableness' Scripture enjoins (Phil. 4:5), Strange provides a model for us all."

> **Sinclair B. Ferguson,** Chancellor's Professor of Systematic Theology, Reformed Theological Seminary; Teaching Fellow, Ligonier Ministries

"Excellent history schools us in wisdom and truth, and *Empowered Witness* is no exception to this rule. Alan Strange skillfully examines the oft-misunderstood but biblical, true doctrine of the spirituality of the church. This book is required reading for anyone who wants to engage the world and at the same time preserve the church's gospel mission."

> **J. V. Fesko,** Harriet Barbour Professor of Systematic and Historical Theology, Reformed Theological Seminary, Jackson

"The fruit of deep reflection over many years, this book by Alan Strange offers the wisdom we need now more than ever. Christ is building his church—his way—and *Empowered Witness* points us in the right direction."

> **Michael Horton,** J. Gresham Machen Professor of Systematic Theology and Apologetics, Westminster Seminary California

"The spirituality of the church is a doctrine that has fallen on hard times in recent years, and perhaps understandably so, given its very real historical association with a laissez-faire attitude to slavery in the antebellum American South. Nonetheless, at its heart, it expresses a vital truth: the church's business is primarily heaven, not earth; yet Christians still live in the earthly city, and our faith is to make a difference in all areas of our lives. In this context, Alan Strange's book is to be heartily welcomed as a guide for the perplexed who seek to honor the church's task in dwelling on heavenly things while using this mindset as a motive for loving neighbors and being a good citizen. It is a tricky and controversial subject, but Strange's thoughtful, clear, and kind book gently threads the needle. I hope it receives a wide readership and generates many constructive discussions."

> **Carl R. Trueman,** Professor of Biblical and Religious Studies, Grove City College; author, *The Rise and Triumph of the Modern Self*

"If the church fails to clearly address the revolutionary cultural and social changes in today's world, it will be a dereliction of duty, but if it identifies itself with any factions in that world, the piercing message of the gospel will be blunted. Alan Strange discusses these topics with great skill and insight, using his encyclopedic knowledge of Charles Hodge's contribution to debates on slavery and the spirituality of the church. This is a book that should inform and shape our thinking; it is not to be missed."

> **Robert Letham,** Senior Research Fellow, Union School of Theology

"As indispensable as Charles Hodge is for the history of American Presbyterianism, Alan Strange contends that Hodge is crucial for its future as well. Hodge steadfastly upheld the church's spiritual vocation in his day—despite criticism from the South and the North in times of both peace and war. Strange, with dispassionate sense and impassioned urgency, calls us to follow Hodge's example in our day and remain steadfast to the church's divine calling, lest we deprive the world of consolation that the church alone can provide."

A. Craig Troxel, Robert G. den Dulk Professor of Practical Theology, Westminster Seminary California; author, *With All Your Heart*

"The spirituality of the church is a crucial doctrine and a rather simple idea, even if it is sometimes challenging to apply. Yet the church can so easily lose sight of this doctrine or simply reject it, especially in times of high political tension. Alan Strange's clear and charitable appeal for the 'mere spirituality of the church' is thus timely and welcome. Contemporary readers would do well to ponder Charles Hodge's wise reflections in the midst of his own politically charged context, and Strange is an excellent guide."

David VanDrunen, Robert B. Strimple Professor of Systematic Theology and Christian Ethics, Westminster Seminary California

"The debate over American slavery and the ensuing Civil War may not seem the best context for revisiting the doctrine of the spirituality of the church, but Alan Strange looks carefully at the teaching of Charles Hodge that was refined and nuanced in his debates with Southern Presbyterians and other competing versions of the doctrine. Though Hodge did not win the day, he points to how the church can speak into the pervasive politicization of our age. Strange's commendation of a 'mere spirituality' is indeed no diminution of the church's voice but rather the more excellent way of an 'empowered witness' to a divided and confused culture."

John R. Muether, Dean of Libraries and Professor of Church History, Reformed Theological Seminary, Orlando

"What should be the role of the church in the affairs of the state, particularly its political process? Alan Strange addresses this much-mooted question primarily through an in-depth treatment—largely sympathetic yet also critical—of Charles Hodge's wrestling for the answer. Following Hodge, Strange offers his own balanced understanding of the spirituality of the church as an institution. His insights will be helpful for Christians today faced with the same difficult question. A valuable read."

Richard B. Gaffin Jr., Professor Emeritus of Biblical and Systematic Theology, Westminster Theological Seminary

Empowered Witness

Empowered Witness

Politics, Culture, and the Spiritual Mission of the Church

Alan D. Strange

Foreword by Kevin DeYoung

:: CROSSWAY®

WHEATON, ILLINOIS

This work draws on the author's dissertation, published originally by P&R as *The Doctrine of the Spirituality of the Church in the Ecclesiology of Charles Hodge*, Reformed Academic Dissertations (Phillipsburg, NJ: P&R, 2017). Used by permission of P&R.
Cover design: Faceout Studio, Tim Green
First printing 2024
Printed in the United States of America

Trade paperback ISBN: 978-1-4335-8427-5
ePub ISBN: 978-1-4335-8430-5
PDF ISBN: 978-1-4335-8428-2

Library of Congress Cataloging-in-Publication Data
Names: Strange, Alan D., author.
Title: Empowered witness : politics, culture, and the spiritual mission of the church / Alan D. Strange ; foreword by Kevin DeYoung.
Description: Wheaton, Illinois : Crossway, 2024. | Includes bibliographical references and index.
Identifiers: LCCN 2023022924 (print) | LCCN 2023022925 (ebook) | ISBN 9781433584275 (trade paperback) | ISBN 9781433584282 (pdf) | ISBN 9781433584305 (epub)
Subjects: LCSH: Mission of the church—History. | Christianity and politics—History. | Christianity and culture—History. | Church and state—History. | Theology, Doctrinal—United States—History. | Great Commission (Bible)
Classification: LCC BV601.8 .S87 2024 (print) | LCC BV601.8 (ebook) | DDC 266—dc23/eng /20230815
LC record available at https://lccn.loc.gov/2023022924
LC ebook record available at https://lccn.loc.gov/2023022925

Crossway is a publishing ministry of Good News Publishers.

To my grandchildren,
Petra, Leo, Gus, and Rosalind

Contents

Foreword

IN THE SUMMER OF 2023, at the General Assembly in Memphis, Tennessee, the Presbyterian Church in America (PCA) celebrated its fiftieth anniversary. As a part of the commemoration, commissioners were given a professionally produced replica of a document titled *A Message to All Churches of Jesus Christ throughout the World from the General Assembly of the National Presbyterian Church*. The document dates from 1973 and was issued at the founding of the PCA (then called the National Presbyterian Church). The *Message to All Churches* was named and written as a conscious echo of a previous document. In 1861, James Henley Thornwell issued his *Address to All Churches of Christ* at the founding of the Presbyterian Church in the Confederate States of America (PCCSA). In fact, the PCA deliberately began as a denomination (in Birmingham, Alabama) on December 4, 1973, because the PCCSA had its beginning (in Augusta, Georgia) on December 4, 1861.

These origins continue to be a source of celebration for some and a source of embarrassment for others. The fact is that the PCA saw itself at its founding—and still sees itself today, in some respects—as a continuing church, as the faithful and orthodox branch of the Southern Presbyterian denomination. And make no mistake, the legacy of Southern Presbyterianism is complex. Take Thornwell, for example. Should he be remembered as a gifted educator, preacher, and writer, as the most influential theologian and churchman of his era? Or should he be remembered as a man who defended slavery and helped give birth to the Confederacy? Undoubtedly, he was all the above.

Because of Thornwell's complicated personal history, Christians in recent decades have been largely dismissive of one of his most strongly held convictions. The first point in Thornwell's inaugural address from 1861 was to explain and defend the spirituality of the church. For most hearers today—including Bible-believing Presbyterians and other conservative Christians—the spirituality of the church means one thing: a wrongheaded and shameful defense of slavery. And it's true, Thornwell and other Presbyterians used the doctrine to support the "peculiar institution" in the South. But it would be a mistake to think the doctrine of the spirituality of the church began in antebellum America as a convenient way to avoid taking a hard look at slavery. The explicit doctrine goes back at least to the Second Book of Discipline (1578) in Scotland, and in seed form it goes back further than that. Even in America, Thornwell was far from the only one to defend the spirituality of the church. Charles Hodge, to cite one important example, believed in a version of the spirituality of the church, even as he took issue with how Thornwell applied the doctrine.

When the PCA began in 1973, it announced its continuing allegiance to the spirituality of the church. Here is how the *Message to All Churches* puts it:

> We believe the Church in its visible aspect is still essentially a spiritual organism. As such, its authority, motivation and power

come from Christ, the Head, who is seated at the right hand of God. He has given us His rulebook for the Church, namely, the Word of God written. We understand the task of the Church to be primarily declarative and ministerial, not legislative or magisterial. It is our duty to set forth what He has given us in His Word and not to devise our own message or legislate our own laws.[1]

This is a good summary of the spirituality of the church. The nature of church power is ministerial and declarative. This means all church power—whether exercised by the whole body, pronounced from the pulpit, or bound up in representative officers—must be in service to Christ (ministerial) and involves stating and enforcing the Word of God (declarative). The church does not have the competence, nor the authority, to make pronouncements on every matter that might matter to men and women. The aims of the church are first and foremost spiritual and eternal. Through most of Reformed history, the spirituality of the church has not entailed a silence on all political matters but rather a commitment to the uniqueness of the church's mission and a principled conviction that the eternal concerns of the church should not be swallowed up by the temporal concerns of the state.

For all these reasons—and many others you will read about in the pages ahead—I am thankful for this book. Alan Strange has marshaled his considerable expertise in this area to write an accessible introduction to the spirituality of the church. Several years ago, I began urging Alan and Crossway to get together and make this book a reality. Now it is finally here; I pray the book finds a wide

1 *Message to All Churches*, PCA Historical Center, December 7, 1973, https://www.pcahistory .org/.

audience. With admirable skill, Alan shows how the spirituality of the church has been used (and abused) throughout history. But more than that, he also makes a compelling case for employing the doctrine in the church today. Don't let the size of the volume fool you. *Empowered Witness* is a learned and important book. While the spirituality of the church will not answer every question pertaining to politics or cultural engagement, it is a historic and biblical doctrine, and we neglect it to our peril.

KEVIN DEYOUNG
June 2023

Acknowledgments

I AM SO GRATEFUL to P&R Publishing for their kind permission to turn the dissertation that I published with them in 2017 (*The Doctrine of the Spirituality of the Church in the Ecclesiology of Charles Hodge*) into this present volume. All who helped with that work are thanked again here.

I want to recognize as well the support of Mid-America Reformed Seminary, which granted me a sabbatical, part of which was used for researching and writing this volume. In addition to colleagues who took up responsibilities for me in the institution during that sabbatical, I am also grateful for the research support of Bart Voskuil and the technical assistance of Rachel Luttjeboer.

I would also like to thank the students, parishioners, and conference attendees (lay, ministerial, and academic) who heard some part of this material for their patience, kindness, and feedback. Many conversations with colleagues, in the academy and the church, also proved helpful. I am particularly grateful to Justin Taylor at Crossway for his encouragement to write this volume and for helping me along the way.

Thanks are due to a number of Justin's coworkers at Crossway, without whom this volume would not have come to pass. I am particularly grateful to and for David Barshinger and the invaluable editorial aid he rendered to me in working on this book. He helped in countless ways and should receive combat pay for all the time that he spent laboring on my manuscript and with the author. I also appreciate editorial help from Amy Kruis as well as the help of Matt Tully, Dan Bush, Kirsten Pott, and Dan Farrell, and those who work with them in Marketing, Sales, Typesetting, and Design, respectively. I'm grateful to work with this remarkable team. For my family, I always give thanks, especially to my ever-supportive wife, without whose assistance and love this book would have been most difficult—as would be all that I do. Even after a serious cancer diagnosis and months of devastating chemotherapy, she continues to encourage me in everything, above all by her unshakable faith in the goodness and love of her Savior.

Amid all this, our first grandchildren were born this year (Petra, Leo, Gus, and Rosalind). Everything that they say about grandkids is true. I don't have words to express my gratefulness for them, but I can dedicate this book to them and pray that, as my family grows in the Lord, the church will increasingly come to recover its spiritual calling.

ALAN D. STRANGE
December 2023

Abbreviations

BRPR	*Biblical Repertory and Princeton Review*
BRTR	*Biblical Repertory and Theological Review*
CHMC	Charles Hodge Manuscript Collection
CHP	Charles Hodge Papers
JPH	*Journal of Presbyterian History*
JSH	*Journal of Southern History*

Introduction

THE CALLING, OR MISSION, of the church as the church is to proclaim the gospel to the ends of the earth, not to be another merely (or even chiefly) political, social, or economic institution. The church, in its full-orbed existence, may have political, economic, or social concerns that develop out of its mission, but those aspects are not what primarily mark and define it. Our Lord Jesus Christ, who is head and King of the church, made it clear in his marching orders to the church—what we've come to call the Great Commission—that he intended the church to go to every people group (often translated "nations") and to evangelize and disciple them (Matt. 28:18–20), enfolding them into his kingdom, which is "not of this world" (John 18:36), a kingdom that does not have the transitory but the eternal at its heart (2 Cor. 4:18). It is Christ himself, our heavenly King—since he is with us even now by his Holy Spirit (1 Cor. 15:45)—who gathers and perfects his church (Westminster Confession of Faith 25.3) through the appointed means.

The gospel is not about worldly success in any proper sense, then, but is rather about deliverance from the penalty, power, and ultimately the presence of sin, a message that comes to permeate the whole of the lives of those transformed by it. We can rightly say that the message of the church is a spiritual one, coming to people of every sort in every land to bring them here and hereafter into the spiritual reality of the kingdom of Christ. Therefore, Paul encourages the Christians in Corinth, "In whatever condition each was called, there let him remain with God" (1 Cor. 7:24). Paul makes clear that the bondservant may and should avail himself of the opportunity of freedom (1 Cor. 7:21). He also makes clear, however, that whatever condition one finds himself in, even whether one is married or not, is not paramount: what is most important is not one's vocation or life circumstance but being called by and coming to Christ, being a new man or woman in Christ. Paul's concern is that his readers are Christians, whatever else may be true of their lives. His concern for them, to put it another way, is chiefly spiritual.

This is the spiritual message that the church is privileged to herald to the world (salvation by grace alone), the good news—the meaning of *gospel*—without which there is no good news. The story of the world after Adam's fall is nothing but bad news since all is sin, darkness, and hopelessness without the good news of the gospel. The gospel of salvation in Christ, however, is the good news that transforms the worst into the best, seen particularly at the cross, where humanity at its worst not only fails to defeat God but where God uses humanity's attempt to do so as the centerpiece of our salvation. Christ has overcome the world. This is the message that the church joyfully preaches to the world. It does not preach itself, nor does it promote some sort of political, social, economic, or cultural utopia to be achieved in this age.

The church preaches that we are to live in this age not for this age but for the coming age that has broken in on this age and beckons us to a new heavens and a new earth that await all who trust in Christ alone. This is no "superspirituality" and certainly not any form of gnosticism but simply the recognition of what is central—the spiritual message of the gospel—out of which all else radiates and from which the full-orbed Christian life, with all its consequences, emerges. This is the great message given to the church to proclaim to the world (faith alone in Christ alone), not some lesser political, social, or economic message that addresses only the things that pertain to this world and not to the world to come.

The gospel is a spiritual message for a world whose greatest need is spiritual: redemption from sin and new life in Christ. This is not to say, however, that the effects of the gospel do not have consequences for the world in which we live. Indeed, the effects of the gospel, when the church obeys the Great Commission and the gospel is taken worldwide, is that the nations, in the comprehensive obedience taught to the faithful, come to have among them those who both trust (fundamentally) and obey (consequentially); thus the Christian faith and its fruits do, in fact, profoundly change the world because those touched by the gospel are new creations and because that spiritual rebirth affects them and those around them.

The task of the church as such is not to transform the world at large or any society in it. The task of the church is to transform lives: to proclaim the gospel as the person and work of Christ applied by the power of the Holy Spirit in the means of grace so that men and women come to Christ by faith and are justified, adopted, and sanctified—all a gift of God's grace. Such changed lives typically affect the lives of others in the various societies in which the saints find themselves. We as God's people, the church, must certainly be ready to give an answer for the hope that we have within (1 Pet. 3:15) to all those we encounter in their profound spiritual need—chiefly, salvation in Jesus Christ. That we are concerned primarily for the spiritual vitality of those around us, however, does not mean that we as Christians are to be indifferent to the nonspiritual needs and sufferings of those around us, but we are to love and help them as we have opportunity, as did the good Samaritan (Luke 10:25–37), a responsibility with implications reflected even in the final judgment (Matt. 25:31–46).

All that constitutes such obedience, however, does not play out in the life of the corporate, or institutional, church. The church can be variously conceived: as an institute, on the one hand, or as an organism, on the other.[1] While it is the mission of the church as institute to evangelize and disciple all her members among the nations of the world, it is not the mission of the church as institute to incarnate the Christian faith in all of life. It is the call of the members of the church as organism to live the whole of their lives from the standpoint of faith and obedience, taking the ethics taught them by the church, for instance, and employing Christian ethics in their businesses, politics, culture, and so on. The church as institute must remain the church, a spiritual entity, and does not become the state, a civil entity, or the family, a biological entity. It does not even seek to do as institute what its members may do, singly or collectively, in the ordinary living of their Christian lives; this latter imperative is the task of the church as organism.[2]

1   Abraham Kuyper, *Collected Works in Public Theology*, vol. 3, *Common Grace: God's Gifts for a Fallen World*, ed. Jordan J. Ballor and J. Daryl Charles, trans. Nelson D. Kloosterman and Ed M. van der Maas (1904; repr., Bellingham, WA: Lexham, 2020), 36–43.

2   In his book *Political Church: The Local Assembly as Embassy of Christ's Rule* (Downers Grove, IL: IVP Academic, 2016), Jonathan Leeman is critical of aspects of this distinction between the church as institute and organism (378–88) and finds more useful distinctions in church polity having to do with the nature of church power (380–82). Like others, Leeman believes that Kuyper ultimately developed his concept of church as organism at the expense of the church as institute. I think Kuyper did have this tendency, though Leeman himself appears

Throughout history, and again in our times, challenges have come from a variety of corners to the church as church—or, as just noted, the church as institute—pushing it to be something that it is not called to be. Some say that if the church is to have any value to society, it must be or become a political, social, or economic entity, as quarters of the church in the United States became in the late nineteenth and early twentieth centuries when figures like Walter Rauschenbusch and Washington Gladden promoted the social gospel.[3] This pressure that the church become like other earthly agencies or institutions stems from the conclusion that some agenda other than the one to which the church is called is really the most important thing in the world.

Marxism or other economic or social ideologies are seen by such who ill-regard the true calling of the church as most needful for the problems that currently beset us. These all-comprehensive ideologies demand that the church, along with the family, the university, the state, and any other institutions, if they are to be worth anything, join them in their conviction, as was Sigmund Freud's, that all reality is sexual/psychological—or, in Karl Marx's case, economic; in Charles Darwin's, biological; and so forth—especially manifested in the fluid genderism left in Freud's wake that outpaces our best attempts to keep up.[4]

---

to consider the "Christian" political position on given issues as more discernible than I do. I think a fair amount of legitimate political differences exists within Reformed confessional bounds.

3   For a favorable view, see Christopher H. Evans, *The Social Gospel in American Religion: A History* (New York: New York University Press, 2017), esp. 107–34. Even when positively presented, the net effect of the social gospel's impact on the churches of the time was, in my view, subversive of the church's true calling.

4   One of the best recent books to illuminate the historical roots of the current sexual crises that confront the church, given the all-pervasive influence of figures like Jean-Jacques Rousseau, William Wordsworth, Friedrich Nietzsche, Sigmund Freud, and others who have shaped

Martin Luther's theology has been portrayed as teaching, "Let God be God!"[5] It is the burden of this book to say, "Let the church be the church." A variety of competing claims threaten to overrun and overwhelm the institutional church in our times. The call of the Lord to the church, the mission that he has given to the church, is an essentially spiritual one. If the church loses that, she has nothing to offer the world, or as D. Martyn Lloyd-Jones reportedly said, "The church does the world the least good when she seeks to be most like it."[6] The world does not need the church to echo all its utopian schemes for a better life. The world needs the church to preach the gospel to it. Yes, when that gospel is faithfully preached and received, men and women throughout the world not only come to Christ but also live in ways that better everything about them. If the church fails to do that, however, as she is called to do it, she suffers and the whole world with her. As attractive as it might seem at any given point for the church to cease to be the truly spiritual body that her Lord calls her to be, it is, in fact, for the church to retreat into futility.

This book, it should be here noted, does not seek to resolve all the difficult problems that surround this subject, such as the relation-

---

contemporary views on gender and various sexual aberrations, is Carl R. Trueman, *The Rise and Triumph of the Modern Self: Cultural Amnesia, Expressive Individualism, and the Road to Sexual Revolution* (Wheaton, IL: Crossway, 2020).

5   Philip S. Watson, *Let God Be God! An Interpretation of the Theology of Martin Luther* (Philadelphia: Muhlenberg, 1949).

6   I heard this quote attributed to D. Martyn Lloyd-Jones many years ago, and though I have searched for the source, I have not been able to find it. This sentiment certainly rings true to what Lloyd-Jones says elsewhere; see D. Martyn Lloyd-Jones, *A First Book of Daily Readings* (Epworth, 1970), excerpted in "April 18 Daily Devotional: *A First Book of Daily Readings,* D. Martyn Lloyd-Jones," Orthodox Presbyterian Church (website), accessed March 22, 2023, https://opc.org/.

ship between church and state or between Christ and culture or the place of public or political theology.[7] For example, two-kingdom advocates distinguish broadly between the redemptive and secular (common) realms, and neo-Calvinists seek to integrate the two.[8] Both approaches arguably have insightful contributions and valid concerns about the other, and these two schools, and variants thereof, can continue to battle for their models and the help that they might bring at various points while agreeing with the central concerns of this book.

Beyond the ham-handed efforts of early twentieth-century social gospelers, who rendered the church another public aid society, albeit a religious one, those interested in political or public theology in more recent decades have generally been more subtle and sophisticated in their attempts to bring their convictions to bear on civil society broadly.[9] Ultimately, however, some have often proved no

7   The classic statement of the relationship of Christ to culture—containing his view of five different stances between Christ and culture, with the Reformed view seen as "Christ the Transformer of Culture"—remains H. Richard Niebuhr, *Christ and Culture* (New York: Harper and Brothers, 1951), 190–229. Many reassessments have occurred over time; two helpful ones include Craig A. Carter, *Rethinking Christ and Culture: A Post-Christendom Perspective* (Grand Rapids, MI: Brazos, 2006); D. A. Carson, *Christ and Culture Revisited* (Grand Rapids, MI: Eerdmans, 2008).

8   David VanDrunen, as a leading two-kingdom proponent, should be consulted, particularly his *Living in God's Two Kingdoms: A Biblical Vision for Christianity and Culture* (Wheaton, IL: Crossway, 2010). For an integrationist attempt in a ministry context, see Timothy Keller, *Center Church: Doing Balanced, Gospel-Centered Ministry in Your City* (Grand Rapids, MI: Zondervan, 2012). For his assessment of Niebuhr's *Christ and Culture* and of a two-kingdom approach, see esp. 194–234.

9   Oliver O'Donovan's books are part of the contemporary movement to engage political theology, especially *The Desire of the Nations: Rediscovering the Roots of Political Theology* (New York: Cambridge University Press, 1996). Another moderating voice in this discussion is James Davison Hunter, *To Change the World: The Irony, Tragedy, and Possibility of Christianity in the Late Modern World* (New York: Oxford University Press, 2010). A recent multiauthor volume that celebrates and expands on Richard Mouw's conviction that "the gospel in its fullness must be directed to all dimensions of human life," from a centrist-left position,

less partisan than the social gospel promoters, who were politically quite liberal. Certainly, many contemporary advocates of political or public theology have tended in progressive directions not likely to garner evangelical support, though some who promote political theology do so from a more moderate position.[10]

We should not, on the one hand, adopt partisan political positions as the church over which those who affirm the same creeds and confessions may rightly differ; we should not, on the other hand, fail to affirm what God's word clearly teaches, even if our proclamation may be perceived to have political impact. Some within the Reformed and Presbyterian world hold to views about the civil reign of King Jesus that have deep historical roots, and various parties continue to vie for some version of Christendom even in an age that has largely been conceded as being post-Christian.[11] Nonetheless, I hope that the most zealous Covenanter can read this book and agree that the church must remain the

---

is Matthew Kaemingk, ed., *Reformed Public Theology: A Global Vision for Life in the World* (Grand Rapids, MI: Baker Academic, 2021), vii.

10 The more moderate position of a James Hunter might be contrasted with a more liberal one of someone like Miroslav Volf, who along with his mentor Jürgen Moltmann, takes things in a direction likely to be seen as partisan left from those on the right. See, for example, Volf's *Exclusion and Embrace: A Theological Exploration of Identity, Otherness, and Reconciliation* (Nashville: Abingdon, 1996); and, more recently, *Flourishing: Why We Need Religion in a Globalized World* (New Haven, CT: Yale University Press, 2015).

11 Probably no Presbyterians are as ardent in all their theocratic convictions as are the Covenanters, a group whose detailed history is found in J. K. Hewison, *The Covenanters: A History of the Church in Scotland from the Reformation to the Revolution*, 2 vols. (1913; repr., Edinburgh: Banner of Truth, 2019). Their influence in America, particularly in opposing slavery and championing the civil kingship of Christ, can be gauged from Joseph S. Moore, *Founding Sins: How a Group of Antislavery Radicals Fought to Put Christ into the Constitution* (New York: Oxford University Press, 2016). James Renwick Willson was a nineteenth-century American Covenanter whose collected articles in *Political Danger: Essays on the Mediatorial Kingship of Christ over Nations and Their Political Institutions, 1809–1838* (Pittsburgh: Crown and Covenant, 2009) provide a biblical and theological rationale for "the crown rights of King Jesus," even in the American disestablishment context.

church and, as such, should not "intermeddle with civil affairs which concern the commonwealth."[12] Some positions would wall off the Christian faith from any influence on the public square. Not this work. Other positions would gladly have the church be viewed as the Republican or Democratic Party at prayer; some progressives and reactionaries, rejecting the "old" politics, look to others now.[13] Again, this work calls for the church to baptize no political party or movement.

I believe that what I propose and what I hope might be welcomed is in keeping with Augustine's seminal insights in *The City of God* (412–426).[14] In the century before Augustine, Constantine was converted (312), and Eusebius, the father of church history, became his court chronicler. Previously, many Christians, who were under persecution, had been chiliasts, expecting the coming of Christ to be followed by a thousand-year reign of Christ on the earth. With the conversion of the emperor, Eusebius identified

---

12 Westminster Confession of Faith 31.4. It should be noted that although chap. 31 has been amended in the American church—the Orthodox Presbyterian Church (OPC) and Presbyterian Church in America (PCA), for instance—this quote (from 31.5 in the original 1647 edition) remains the same, both in the original version and in the amended American version.

13 Stephen Wolfe, *The Case for Christian Nationalism* (Moscow, ID: Canon, 2022), is a confused and disturbing politicizing work. Kevin DeYoung's trenchant review addresses its primary problems: "The Rise of Right-Wing Wokeism—Review: *The Case for Christian Nationalism* by Stephen Wolfe," The Gospel Coalition, November 28, 2022, https://www.thegospel coalition.org/. DeYoung's review is more balanced on the "nationalism" question than the book by Andrew L. Whitehead and Samuel L. Perry, *Taking America Back for God: Christian Nationalism in the United States* (New York: Oxford University Press, 2020), which rightly raises an alarm about Christian nationalism but in a way that reveals its own liberal biases and shortcomings.

14 For a discussion of Augustinian insight in properly distinguishing the church from the Roman Empire, see Alan D. Strange, *The Doctrine of the Spirituality of the Church in the Ecclesiology of Charles Hodge*, Reformed Academic Dissertations (Phillipsburg, NJ: P&R, 2017), 8–15. This is my published dissertation and will hereafter be referred to as *Spirituality of the Church*. Much of this current work relies on my work in my dissertation.

the church with the state and saw a future golden age in which the Roman state and church would triumph and together dominate the whole world.

When Rome was sacked by Alaric and the Visigoths in 410 and other evidence of the empire's dissolution accrued, Augustine addressed the theological crisis by writing *The City of God*. In response to the charge that the church waxed at the expense of the waning state, he pointed out the failures of paganism and made clear that the church was its own entity, not to be simply identified with the Roman Empire—or any other empire, for that matter. Augustine wrote to assure Christians that though Rome may fall, the church will never fall but will continue to carry out its task until that great day of the Lord. The book in your hands is in the spirit of such Augustinian reasoning.

Consonant with that Augustinian conviction, I do not seek to muzzle the prophetic voice of the church against such injustices as abortion, racism, abuse of power, and denial of due process in the course of the church's proclamation of the whole counsel of God. The church must, in all its ministries, declare God's word and minister to the spiritual welfare of those in and out of the church. We do not need less of a Christian witness in the public square; we need more of one. This is evidenced not only in the writings of those on the political left or right, who would bring biblical insight into play more explicitly in the public square, but also in the writings of some two-kingdom thinkers like David VanDrunen, who, in his book on politics, brings Christian wisdom and insight to bear (under a natural-law rubric) on the public square in a variety of ways.[15]

---

15 David VanDrunen, *Politics after Christendom: Political Theology in a Fractured World* (Grand Rapids, MI: Zondervan Academic, 2020).

We do not need more of the secularism of the French Revolution sort, marked as it was by viciousness. Nor do we need the visible institutional church to be swamped with and give way to political concerns. We need the church to remain and be the church, both for its own welfare and that of the world. All Reformed and Presbyterian churches affirm Calvin's second use of the law—as a guide for society broadly—and when civil government refuses to recognize God's law explicitly, we pray that it will do so in spite of such unbelief because the works of the law are written on the rulers' hearts (Rom. 2:14–15).[16]

This book, then, seeks to refocus the church on its proper calling and mission, encouraging it to be what Christ has called it to be and not to give way to political concerns, as is so tempting and so common. This work seeks to foster a kind of "mere spirituality," with apologies to C. S. Lewis, that would obtain in the face of competing models for understanding state and church, Christ and culture, faith and politics, and the like. In other words, I call on all Reformed and Presbyterians—indeed, all Protestants—however they conceive the relations of church and state, faith and politics, and so on, to embrace the "mere spirituality of the church." At the same time, this approach will clash with that of those determined, on either left or right (however they may self-identify), to organize the church according to their own political convictions.

All persons have political convictions, and those of the Christian must be consonant with Scripture, as all his beliefs must be. This does not mean, however, that those views should be preached as gospel truth in the pulpit. Yes, one may properly preach, as warranted by the text, that abortion is sin (or that greedy business

16 John Calvin, *Institutes of the Christian Religion*, ed. John T. McNeill, trans. Ford Lewis Battles, Library of Christian Classics (Philadelphia: Westminster, 1960), 2.7.10.

practices, racism, same-sex marriage, oppressive exploitation, and so on are wrong) but not what precise political moves should be made to address it. To preach against sin is one thing; to preach the detailed solution to complex political questions, especially about which people of the same confession differ, is another.

This book examines, first, the doctrine of *the spirituality of the church*—that is, the call, task, or mission of the institutional church. It then surveys that doctrine particularly as it developed stateside in the nineteenth century, especially as it relates to the nation's enthrallment to slavery. We will see that Charles Hodge of Princeton Theological Seminary opposed the doctrine of the spirituality of the church as he initially saw it brought forth by James Henley Thornwell and others, particularly at the 1859 and 1860 General Assemblies of the Presbyterian Church, but modified it for his own purposes in opposition to the Gardiner Spring Resolutions at the 1861 General Assembly. The Presbyterian Church, turning away from the spirituality of the church, ultimately came to embrace an approach to political and civil matters that overwhelmed the spiritual: Northern Presbyterianism took actions during and following the US Civil War (1861–1865), including the reunion of the Old and New Schools on an unsound doctrinal and polity basis, that compromised the church and led her into theological liberalism.

The Presbyterian Church, as a great cautionary tale, lost its spiritual way in the late nineteenth and early twentieth centuries; since then, mainline Presbyterianism has suffered the loss of the spirituality of the church, pervasive politicization, and arguably, because of that, precipitous decline.[17] In the face of the widespread

---

17 Even after unions with other significant bodies in 1958 and 1983, membership in the Presbyterian Church (USA) plummeted from a high of 4.25 million in 1965 to a low of

decline of this doctrine, recent years have witnessed a welcome awareness of the historical abuse of the spirituality of the church among confessionally sound Reformed and Presbyterian churches that once imbibed this doctrine.[18] While it is true that it was abused in some measure, such abuse does not mean that the doctrine has no proper use.[19] It is the aim of this book to warn against dismissing the spirituality of the church altogether just because it has been historically abused and to observe that if it is shelved, the church will suffer from losing a proper doctrine of the church's spiritual mission. This book seeks to address both the abuse and the neglect of the spirituality of the church and to call for a healthy return to a mere spirituality, one that does not dodge painful responsibilities but remains alert and sensitive to the temptation of politicizing the institutional church.

1.19 million at the end of 2021. During all this hemorrhaging, the mainline Presbyterian Church became more politically progressive, and politics became paramount. Rick Jones, "PC(USA) 2021 Statistics Continue to Show Declining Membership," Office of the General Assembly, Presbyterian Church (USA), April 25, 2022, https://www.pcusa.org/.

18 Sean Michael Lucas deals with the use and abuse of the spirituality of the church in the Southern Presbyterian Church, both in its earlier and later forms. *For a Continuing Church: The Roots of the Presbyterian Church in America* (Phillipsburg, NJ: P&R, 2015), 39–65, 101–34. Jemar Tisby understandably finds this doctrine problematic and rightly points out how selectively it was used. *The Color of Compromise: The Truth about the American Church's Complicity in Racism* (Grand Rapids, MI: Zondervan, 2019), 85–87. Tisby also, writing after the death of George Floyd and the protests that followed, finds attempts, historical and still ongoing, to justify racism in Presbyterian and other churches. *How to Fight Racism: Courageous Christianity and the Journey toward Racial Justice* (Grand Rapids, MI: Zondervan Reflective, 2021), 97–103 passim. I agree that the spirituality of the church, lamentably, has and can be used for excusing racism and other sins. This work calls for a better way, one that fully embraces what the Scripture teaches on every subject, including its condemnation of racism, without inviting or allowing the church to give way to pervasive politicization.

19 The principle of *abusus non tollit usum* (the abuse of a thing does not preclude its [proper] use) is fundamental in ecclesiology and church polity. In our current atmosphere of rejecting any practice that has ever been abused, the principle that "abuse does not mean no proper use" must be retained, or much will be lost.

This book presses for a mere spirituality that encourages the church as church to mind its spiritual business and not to seek to proclaim anything but "Thus says the Lord" and what may be rightly implied from Scripture. The church as church lacks the competency and the authority to address political situations in detail because it lacks the scriptural word to opine about specific proposed remedies such as higher minimum wages, better tax schemes, term limits for public office, and many other matters that should be decided in the political forum and not in the ecclesiastical one. This is what this book means when it speaks of the spiritual call that pertains to the church, a call that challenges the church neither simply to become the world by echoing its highest humanism nor to flee from the world and retreat into a holy huddle. Rather, the church must be what Christ has called her to be, both for her own good and for the world's, all to the glory and eternal praise of our triune God.[20]

---

20 Alan D. Strange, "The Spirituality of the Church and Her 'Painful Responsibilities,'" in *New Perspectives on Old Princeton*, ed. Kevin DeYoung, Paul Kjoss Helseth, and David P. Smith (London: Routledge, forthcoming).

1

The Doctrine of the
Spirituality of the Church

THE CHURCH'S SPIRITUAL MISSION, or *the spirituality of the church*, is a doctrine that the church has forgotten as a concept or remembered only for its abuses in protecting American slavery and thus, understandably, rejected. I think that the spirituality of the church, however, is something we need to recapture in our dialogue about the church and its mission. Rightly defined, the spirituality of the church applies not only to those who have a particular view of the church and culture but to any conception of the church that understands it as an institution with a distinct spiritual calling that it and only it can perform: this I call *mere spirituality*. If the church fails to see that and tries to be something else—merely another social, political, or economic actor—then what the church is meant to be and to give away is lost, and we are all the poorer for it.

The phrase *the spirituality of the church* may strike many readers as curious. At the same time, the terms *Christian spirituality* and *spiritual theology* are likely familiar to many. Readers might have some idea of what *spirituality* in broader terms means, but having never heard the nomenclature *the spirituality of the church*, they may be left scratching their heads about this term. I hope to show that these concepts—Christian spirituality and the spirituality of the church—are not wholly unrelated, even as I demonstrate that what is referred to as *the spirituality of the church* is addressing something rather distinctive.

The doctrine, though of ancient origins,[1] did not appear in the form of the phrase *the spirituality of the church* until the 1850s in the Old School Presbyterian Church in America (which came into being in 1837 and reunited with the New School in 1869). I address some of this later in the book, especially focusing on that context (1840s–late 1860s), in which we see that the doctrine concerns the province of the church and the nature and limits of its power, specifically the contention that since the church is a spiritual institution, its focus should be spiritual, not civil or political. Though Old School Presbyterians rather widely held convictions about the spirituality of the church, at least the principle that the church is a spiritual kingdom, how to *apply* the principle engendered enormous controversy among them.

Christian Spirituality and the Church

Before plunging into the internecine battles among Old School Presbyterians in applying this doctrine, a short reflection on the nexus between *Christian spirituality* and *the spirituality of the church* might be helpful. Many have employed the term *Christian spirituality*, especially in recent years, to distinguish the theology of the Christian church from the lived experience of the Christian faith.

1 For an extensive treatment of church, state, and their relationships in the biblical, ancient, medieval, and Reformational worlds, see especially Strange, *Spirituality of the Church*, chap. 1.

The spirituality of the church highlights that the church, as the mystical body of Christ filled with the Holy Spirit, is a spiritual rather than a civil entity. The broader notion of *Christian spirituality* has to do with the specific ways in which the Christian life is lived, particularly with respect to Christian devotional practices, the spiritual disciplines that mark the Christian life, whether public or private.[2] Here one may think of, for example, the prayer life of the Christian. This would be a part of what is called *Christian spirituality* and could be set over against the devotional practices of a Muslim or a Buddhist (and thus we may speak of Islamic spirituality or Buddhist spirituality).[3]

How exactly, though, is the broader concept of spirituality connected with the narrower concept of the spirituality of the church? As noted above, spirituality broadly has to do with the spiritual aspects of the Christian life. These spiritual aspects, in Christian theology, are authored by the Holy Spirit, the third person of the blessed, holy, undivided Trinity. Paul identifies the spiritual person as one in whom the Holy Spirit has worked (1 Cor. 2:1–16). The spiritual person is one who enjoys union with Christ and has the

---

2 This is a vast field with sources ranging from the late Henri Nouwen (who wrote more than three dozen books on Christian spirituality) to books on Christian mysticism, histories of Christian spirituality (especially those of Bernard McGinn, whose three-volume *Christian Spirituality* [New York: Crossroad, 1987] and four-volume *Foundations of Mysticism* [New York: Crossroad, 1995] cover the field), and books on the spiritual disciplines by popular authors such as Richard Foster. Christians from the Far East have often contributed to this field, seen in a book like Simon Chan's *Spiritual Theology: A Systematic Study of the Christian Life* (Downers Grove, IL: InterVarsity Press, 1998), in which he treats the question in two parts: the theological principles of spiritual theology and the practices of spiritual theology, addressing under the latter rubric prayer, spiritual exercises focusing on God and self, the word of God, and the world, as well as the rule of life, the discernment of spirits, and the art of spiritual direction.

3 Spirituality in the world religions, including Christianity, receives due attention in the magisterial eighteen-volume set *World Spirituality: An Encyclopedic History of the Religious Quest*, ed. Ewert Cousins (New York: Crossroad, 1985–).

mind of Christ in and by the power of the Holy Spirit. The Holy Spirit authors and fosters Christian spirituality.[4] The spirituality of the church ties in with this thinking because the church is a spiritual entity, a corporate body of those in whom the Spirit has worked. It is this spiritual aspect of the life of the church that determines the nature, exercise, and extent of its power: a spiritual power exercised in a spiritual manner within a spiritual realm.[5] Thus, all sorts of organic connections exist between spirituality broadly conceived and the spirituality of the church properly.

Recent Studies and Historical Perspective

The doctrine of the spirituality of the church is something that has received revived attention in recent years. For instance, D. G. Hart and John Muether, historians in the Orthodox Presbyterian Church, have reintroduced the doctrine, writing,

> Unlike some Reformed theologians who have posited a basic harmony between church and state in the execution of God's sovereignty, American Presbyterianism has also nurtured an understanding of society that stresses fundamental differences

4   The word *spirituality* is often nowadays pitted against *religion*, so that one commonly reads that someone who is no practitioner of "organized religion" is nonetheless "a very spiritual person." Presumably, the inward is identified with spirituality and the outward with religion. Adhering to religion, then, is taken as merely outward and thus inherently hypocritical. In this schema, spirituality is perfectly acceptable because it's an inward virtue that does not have or require outward observances.

5   This is widely recognized in Presbyterian books of church order. For example, see *The Book of Church Order of the Presbyterian Church in America* (Lawrenceville, GA: Office of the Stated Clerk of the General Assembly of the Presbyterian Church in America, 2022), preface (esp. sec. 2, "Preliminary Principles"); part 1, chap. 3 ("The Nature and Extent of Church Power"); and also *The Book of Church Order of the Orthodox Presbyterian Church*, "Form of Government" (Willow Grove, PA: Committee on Christian Education of the Orthodox Presbyterian Church, 2020), chap. 3 ("The Nature and Exercise of Church Power").

between the aims and task of the church and the purpose of the state, [affirming a doctrine] [s]ometimes called the doctrine of the Spirituality of the Church.[6]

In a more recent book, Bryan Estelle addresses many of the themes of this volume from a two-kingdom perspective, and he develops a comprehensive argument calling for a new or renewed commitment to the "primary" mission of the church, which he sees as decidedly spiritual.[7]

This present volume, being more of a survey of American Presbyterian history, relies on the scriptural exegesis of other works, such as Estelle's work or Kevin DeYoung and Greg Gilbert's similar volume on the mission of the church.[8] Additionally, as noted earlier, this book does not generally address the models developed to deal with Christianity and culture and the like except in passing; one of the best-balanced treatments of the two-kingdom question is Jonathon Beeke's *Duplex Regnum Christi*.[9] Relatedly, a good general examination of a Christian approach to politics and its proper nature and limits is David Innes's work.[10] I happily admit,

6   D. G. Hart and John R. Muether, "The Spirituality of the Church," *Ordained Servant* 7, no. 3 (1998): 64. See also Hart and Muether, *Seeking a Better Country: 300 Years of American Presbyterianism* (Phillipsburg, NJ: P&R, 2007), 138–43.

7   Bryan D. Estelle, *The Primary Mission of the Church: Engaging or Transforming the World?* (Fearn, Ross-shire, Scotland: Mentor, 2022). It should be noted that because of the liability tied to the nomenclature *spirituality of the church*, Estelle tends to use other language to describe this doctrine. Other writers have understandably done the same in recent years.

8   Kevin DeYoung and Greg Gilbert, *What Is the Mission of the Church? Making Sense of Social Justice, Shalom, and the Great Commission* (Wheaton, IL: Crossway, 2011).

9   Jonathon D. Beeke, *Duplex Regnum Christi: Christ's Twofold Kingdom in Reformed Theology* (Leiden: Brill, 2021). A few volumes are also quite critical of a two-kingdom approach, perhaps one of the more severe being Willem J. Ouweneel, *The World Is Christ's: A Critique of Two Kingdoms Theology* (Toronto: Ezra Press, 2017).

10 David C. Innes, *Christ and the Kingdoms of Men: Foundations of Political Life* (Phillipsburg, NJ: P&R, 2019).

as a convinced Protestant of the Reformed stripe, that Scripture, not tradition, and thus not the history of the church, is normative. We ultimately go to God's word to develop our doctrine of the mission of the church and to understand what its spirituality should look like.[11]

I would argue, however, that surveying history is quite important in a matter like this: while recognizing that the Bible alone is prescriptive for our doctrine, we nonetheless appreciate the significance that the descriptive living out of our doctrine provides us, which is what we witness in history. Since the spirituality of the church has much to do with church polity—the integrity of the church as an institution vis-à-vis other institutions like the state—and since polity in Reformed and Presbyterian theological studies has developed as a discipline in the field of church history, it is especially fitting to examine church history as we study the spirituality of the church.[12] This book, then, looks at the doctrine of the spirituality of the church in American church history, particularly in the lead-up to and aftermath of the US Civil War, especially as worked out in the ecclesiology of Old School American Presbyterianism.

Though the doctrine of the spirituality of the church has its roots in the seventeenth-century Scottish doctrine of the "spiritual independency of the church" and in the Scottish Second Book of

11 Another clear and helpful book that has implications for the spiritual mission of the church is Guy Prentiss Waters, *How Jesus Runs the Church* (Phillipsburg, NJ: P&R, 2011).

12 For a detailed outworking of the relationship between the history of the church and its polity, see the ongoing serialization of my "Commentary on the Form of Government of the Orthodox Presbyterian Church" and "Commentary on the Book of Discipline of the Orthodox Presbyterian Church," begun in April 2020, in the online office bearers' journal of the Orthodox Presbyterian Church (OPC), *Ordained Servant Online*, at https://www.opc.org/os.html.

Discipline (1578),[13] it was in the American context preceding and during the US Civil War that this doctrine took on a special role in the church's understanding of itself, allowing the church to retain its God-ordained witness to the world without being overwhelmed by the world's concerns and agenda. How some of those difficult waters were navigated, both successfully and not, might suggest to us in our own times how we in the institutional church might make sure that we properly engage the world without being swamped with its concerns and politicized along with so many other institutions.

This present volume, then, while not engaging in extensive biblical exegesis or treating certain important questions connected to the topic under consideration, takes another look at the doctrine of the spirituality of the church especially by considering how the great nineteenth-century Princeton Theological Seminary theologian Charles Hodge used and modified the doctrine. Some who seek to recover the doctrine of the spirituality of the church do so more in keeping with how it was used by some of Hodge's fellow Old School Presbyterians: the border state champion of spirituality, Stuart Robinson, and the dean of Southern Presbyterianism, James Henley Thornwell.[14] Part of the aim of this book is to assess whether Robinson and Thornwell are sound exemplars of the spirituality

---

13 Strange, *Spirituality of the Church*, 23–31.

14 Two good examples of conventional reliance on Thornwell (and Robinson, more recently) include David VanDrunen, *Natural Law and the Two Kingdoms: A Study in the Development of Reformed Social Thought* (Grand Rapids, MI: Eerdmans, 2010), 247–66; Darryl Hart, *A Secular Faith: Why Christianity Favors the Separation of Church and State* (Chicago: Ivan R. Dee, 2006), 117–19. Craig Troxel commends Robinson's spirituality of the church in his foreword to a reprinting of Robinson's 1858 *The Church of God as an Essential Element of the Gospel* (Willow Grove, PA: Committee on Christian Education of the Orthodox Presbyterian Church, 2009), 5–12. And Brian T. Wingard commends Thornwell's in " 'As the Lord Puts Words in Her Mouth': The Supremacy of Scripture in the Ecclesiology of James Henley Thornwell and Its Influence upon the Presbyterian Churches of the South" (PhD diss., Westminster Theological Seminary, 1992).

of the church. It is my contention that Hodge's moderate view of the doctrine expresses it better and is more suitable for recovery and use in our times.

Charles Hodge on the Spirituality of the Church

Hodge's doctrine of the spirituality of the church received no sustained attention until recently, in my dissertation.[15] Hodge was arguably the most influential Old School Presbyterian of the nineteenth century, laboring for more than fifty-five years at its flagship seminary, Princeton Theological Seminary (founded in 1812). Hodge was Princeton's leading professor during the middle part of the nineteenth century, especially enjoying broad influence as the editor of the *Biblical Repertory and Princeton Review*, in which pages he annually gave a detailed analysis of the General Assembly of the Old School Presbyterian Church, an interpretive task that multiplied his influence in the church. Hodge, along with his fellow Princetonians, was seen as the quintessential moderate, and it is no different when it comes to the doctrine of the spirituality of the church.

Robinson, Thornwell, and others were on one end of the spectrum, the radical spirituality of the church wing, we might call it. Others in the Old School Church, especially as the US Civil War intensified, were on the other end of the spectrum, not heedful of the doctrine of the spirituality of the church, only too ready to have the church make political pronouncements, particularly at the General Assemblies of 1861 and 1865, as we will see below. Hodge rejected both extremes and developed a doctrine of the spirituality of the church that was supple and practical. And for Hodge, his doctrine developed out of his overall doctrine of the church, which

---

15   Strange, *Spirituality of the Church*.

he saw as a spiritual institution, a body gathered by the Spirit and given expression in the visible institutional church.

For Hodge, as for Protestants more broadly, the church was in its essence invisible, the visible church being the necessary outward expression of the inward reality of the work of the Spirit. Hodge viewed the church as a spiritual institution that carried out its tasks in spiritual, not political or civil, ways: this was a given that he contended for and developed throughout the whole of his theology. This work, then, examines the doctrine of the spiritual calling of the church especially as it plays out in the doctrine of the spirituality of the church in Charles Hodge's theology. By looking at Hodge particularly, I seek to demonstrate that he developed his doctrine of the church's spirituality in a subtle and nuanced fashion that permitted him to distinguish the church from the state and its political concerns while also allowing the church to retain a prophetic voice in society.

How successful Hodge was in developing his doctrine of the spirituality of the church and how well such an approach served in his day—and would serve in ours, for those seeking to repristinate the doctrine of Hodge or others—remains a challenge, particularly in our pluralistic culture. Some might argue that the spirituality of the church is precisely what a pluralistic society needs: a church that minds its spiritual business and does not disturb a secularized culture that does not want the church to have a public theology. Others would see the spirituality of the church as a failure on the part of a church that has privatized and refuses to call its society to repentance, as the Old School Presbyterian Church arguably failed to call America to repent of slavery.

If this doctrine kept the American Presbyterian Church from fully addressing what many would regard as the greatest evil of its day, what good was it? Other American Christians did not believe that something called the spirituality of the church restrained them from denouncing slavery, and they denounced it in biblical terms. William Wilberforce, to cite a key non-American, condemned slavery on the basis of Christian principles. It should be noted, however, that Wilberforce did so not as a preacher in the pulpit but as a parliamentarian working for abolitionist legislation. In any case, slavery in Britain suffered defeat in no small measure because of the explicitly Christian opposition of Wilberforce and his allies.

At the same time, one might argue that the spirituality of the church tends to keep the church from being overwhelmed by the world's concerns or its agenda. It helps the church maintain its identity as church, distinct from the culture around it. J. Gresham Machen, twentieth-century successor to Hodge at Princeton Seminary, lamented the loss of this distinction, which stemmed from the loss of any sense of the church's spiritual mission. He wrote,

> Weary with the conflicts of the world, one goes into the Church to seek refreshment for the soul. And what does one find? Alas, too often, one finds only the turmoil of the world. The preacher comes forward, not out of a secret place of meditation and power, not with the authority of God's Word permeating his message, not with human wisdom pushed far into the background by the glory of the Cross, but with human opinions about the social problems of the hour or easy solutions of the vast problem of sin.
>
> Is there no refuge from strife? Is there no place of refreshing where a man can prepare for the battle of life? Is there no place where two or three can gather in Jesus' name, to forget for the moment all those things that divide nation from nation and

race from race, to forget human pride, to forget the passions of war, to forget the puzzling problems of industrial strife, and to unite in overflowing gratitude at the foot of the Cross? If there be such a place, then that is the house of God and that the gate of heaven. And from under the threshold of that house will go forth a river that will revive the weary world.[16]

Machen's plea is for a church that knows its spiritual calling and properly understands that it is not the world and that it does the world no good by aping it.

The danger always exists that the church ceases to be the distinct spiritual institution that it is and becomes an adjunct to the society about it. But there is also another danger—that the church becomes a ghetto that shelters its members and renders ineffectual its gospel witness. Can the church concern itself with its own "spirituality" so much that it fails in its mission to the world? It is the contention of this book that as Hodge did when he developed his doctrine of the spirituality of the church, but hopefully better, we can steer a course between the Scylla of the marginalization and irrelevance of the church and the Charybdis of its politicization.

Since mention of the spirituality of the church is largely absent until Hodge's time, one might think that the doctrine is an invention of nineteenth-century American Presbyterianism. After all, the specific term first appears shortly before the US Civil War.[17]

---

16 J. Gresham Machen, *Christianity and Liberalism* (1923; repr., Grand Rapids, MI: Eerdmans, 1994), 179–80.

17 It shows up in the debates between Charles Hodge and James Henley Thornwell and in Stuart Robinson's work, as noted above, regarding the nature of church power, extraecclesiastical Christian societies, and the boards of the Presbyterian Church, particularly at the Presbyterian Church in the United States of America (PCUSA) General Assemblies of 1859 and 1860, reflected in Hodge, *Discussions in Church Polity* (1878; repr., New York: Westminster, 2001),

The idea, particularly as used by Charles Hodge, has to do with what might be called the "province of the church"—the nature and limits of its power—especially its role as an institution over against that of the state. And that concept has roots dating back to the early centuries of the church. This book intends to show that for Hodge these broader uses link up with his particular usage of the spirituality of the church: Hodge saw the church as a spiritual institution, a kingdom "not of this world," gathered and perfected by the Holy Spirit.[18] Hence the spirituality of the church for Hodge came particularly to reflect this reality: the church is a body gathered by the Holy Spirit, over against other societal institutions that are biological (the family) or civil (the state).

Spirituality in the Nineteenth Century Briefly Defined

Recent scholars have been skeptical about when the doctrine of the spirituality of the church developed. Historian Jack Maddex, for instance, notes that "all writers have agreed . . . that Southern Presbyterians embraced 'the spirituality of the church' before 1861."[19] Maddex insists on a different time line:

100–106, 118–33, and in Thornwell, *Collected Writings*, vol. 4 (1875; repr., Carlisle, PA: Banner of Truth, 1974), 145–295.

18 The reference here—that Christ has a "kingdom not of this world"—is from John 18:36, and the Greek is instructive. It reads *ek tou kosmou toutou* ("out of this world" or "from this world"), and the implication is not so much that there are two kingdoms as such (a civil and a spiritual kingdom)—at least that is not the implication of this passage (I make no pretense to address the question of "two kingdoms" such as we would find in Martin Luther or John Calvin, for example)—but that Christ's kingdom does not come out of, emerge from, or rely on the kind of kingdom that Pilate bears rule in, one that bears a sword. Rather, the quality of this kingdom is of a different sort than that of the world from which it does not come. One may translate (as does the RSV) *basileia* as "kingship," so that Jesus is proclaiming that the authority of his kingship is not derived from or reliant on any earthly kingdom but, by contrast, has origins not in or from this world, transcending this present cosmos.

19 Jack P. Maddex, "From Theocracy to Spirituality: The Southern Presbyterian Reversal on Church and State," *JPH* 54, no. 4 (1976): 438. One of Thornwell's leading biographers,

It is time to challenge that generally-accepted premise. Ante-bellum Southern Presbyterians did not teach absolute separa-tion of religion from politics, or even church from state. Most of them were proslavery social activists who worked through the church to defend slavery and reform its practice. Their Confederate militance did not violate any antebellum tradition of pietism. Only during Reconstruction, in drastically altered circumstances, did they take up the cause of a non-secular church—borrowing it from conservative Presbyterians in the border states.[20]

Maddex, I contend, is both right and wrong. He is right that Presbyterians in the South (and in the North, for that matter) before the US Civil War did not teach an absolute separation of religion from politics[21] and also that Reconstruction Southerners were particularly influenced by certain border state Presbyterians (like Stuart Robinson in Kentucky).[22] He is wrong, however, to assert that the doctrine of the spirituality of the church is not only termi-nologically but conceptually a novel idea invented by Southerners in Reconstruction. The notion of the spirituality of the church in some sense extends back through the entire history of the church,

James O. Farmer Jr., is in essential concord with Maddex; see Farmer, *The Metaphysical Confederacy: James Henley Thornwell and the Synthesis of Southern Values* (Macon, GA: Mercer University Press, 1986), 258–61.

20 Maddex, "From Theocracy to Spirituality," 438–39.

21 A point made forcefully in the excellent collection of sermons preached before and during the Civil War, *"God Ordained This War": Sermons on the Sectional Crisis, 1830–1865*, ed. David B. Chesebrough (Columbia: University of South Carolina Press, 1991).

22 Robinson, as noted above, published before the Civil War his great work arguing for his version of the spirituality of the church: *The Church of God as an Essential Element of the Gospel, and the Idea, Structure, and Functions Thereof* (Philadelphia: Joseph M. Wilson, 1858). This work became greatly influential in the South after the war when Robinson joined and served as an early moderator of the Southern Presbyterian Church.

even to biblical times.[23] It is the contention of this work that not only did the concept of the spirituality of the church precede the nineteenth century but also that it was used for something other than supporting slavery, as seen in the case of Charles Hodge.[24]

While some who adduced the spirituality of the church did intend thereby to silence the church from criticizing slavery, this was not Hodge's approach. Hodge's more careful and modest use of the doctrine restricted the church from purely political involvement, while permitting some civil engagement. He asserted that the church has a proper interest in addressing issues that may have civil implications, like Sabbath observance, the place of religion in public education, and slavery.[25] In fine, Hodge maintained that though the church ought not to concern itself with the purely political, at the same time it ought not to restrict itself in addressing matters treated by the Bible simply because such issues may have certain civil or political ramifications. Where to draw the lines— between spiritual and civil, between church and state—is, Hodge acknowledged, "an exceedingly complicated and difficult subject."[26]

23 A recent work by a leading Reformed Old Testament professor well establishes the biblical basis of, inter alia, the spirituality of the church: Estelle, *Primary Mission of the Church*, esp. 47–145. See also Strange, *Spirituality of the Church*, chap. 1.

24 Ernest Trice Thompson also argues that the doctrine of the spirituality of the church was a novelty invented by the Southern church to evade the issue of slavery and to separate faith and politics. See both his magisterial (and still indispensable) three-volume set *Presbyterians in the South* (Richmond, VA: John Knox, 1963–1973) and his smaller work *The Spirituality of the Church: A Distinctive Doctrine of the Presbyterian Church in the United States* (Richmond, VA: John Knox, 1961). E. Brooks Holifield also takes the position that the spirituality of the church served as a cover during the slavery controversy and that the Presbyterian Church in the South otherwise "never truly abstained from social comment." *The Gentlemen Theologians: American Theology in Southern Culture, 1795–1860* (Durham, NC: Duke University Press, 1978), 154.

25 Strange, *Spirituality of the Church*, chaps. 4–5.

26 Charles Hodge, "Relation of the Church and State," *Biblical Repertory and Princeton Review* (hereafter cited as *BRPR*) 35, no. 4 (1863): 679.

Given the brevity of this book, much that is helpful to a full consideration of the subject at hand must be treated lightly or passed over altogether. Thus, for the fuller treatment of matters like the biblical and historical development of both church and state, considered separately and in their mutual relations, I refer the interested reader to my underlying dissertation.[27] Additionally, matters pertaining to Hodge's life and the development of his theology[28]—particularly his doctrine of the Holy Spirit (pneumatology) and his doctrine of the church (ecclesiology), which combine and find a special focus in his doctrine of the spirituality of the church—enjoy due and greater treatment in the larger volume.[29] Especially important in a fuller treatment of these matters is to show how the doctrine of the work of the Holy Spirit (following the long-established understanding of the person of the Holy Spirit) developed in the corpus of John Calvin, "the theologian of the Holy Spirit."[30]

Hodge and his fellows at Princeton rightly lay claim to being theologians of the Holy Spirit as well, seeing the Spirit's application of Christ's purchased redemption to his people as key in understanding the nature of the church and why the church is a spiritual institution, over against the family as a biological one and the state as a civil one. We are going to proceed from this point in our narrative to the question of slavery and how the doctrine of the spirituality of the church interfaced with that, frankly, horrific institution. It should not be assumed, however, that the sort of things briefly described in these last paragraphs may simply be

27 Strange, *Spirituality of the Church*, chap. 1.
28 Strange, *Spirituality of the Church*, chap. 2.
29 Strange, *Spirituality of the Church*, chaps. 3–4.
30 Strange, *Spirituality of the Church*, 132–36.

taken for granted. Interested readers should consult chapters 1–4 of my published dissertation for the deeper questions of church, state, the Holy Spirit, ecclesiology, polity, and the like that go into making up the question of the church's spirituality and its consequent spiritual mission and calling.

2

Slavery and the Spirituality
of the Church

THE ORIGINS AND EARLY DEVELOPMENT of the doctrine of the
spirituality of the church in its modern form, especially in Scotland, had nothing to do with the institution of American slavery.[1]
In the American context, however, particularly in the nineteenth
century, the doctrine of the spirituality of the church came to be
inextricably intertwined with the institution of slavery. Some, such
as James Henley Thornwell and Stuart Robinson, invoked the doctrine to defend the institution and to inure it from fundamental
criticism.[2] Charles Hodge opposed this usage of the spirituality

---

1 Slavery, a monumental subject and concern, particularly in the history of the West, has
   received much attention. I have long been influenced by David Brion Davis, especially *The
   Problem of Slavery in Western Culture* (Ithaca, NY: Cornell University Press, 1966). See also
   his *In the Image of God: Religion, Moral Values, and Our Heritage of Slavery* (New Haven,
   CT: Yale University Press, 2001), and *Inhuman Bondage: The Rise and Fall of Slavery in the
   New World* (New York: Oxford University Press, 2006).

2 Thornwell defended slavery in *Collected Writings*, vol. 4 (1875; repr., Carlisle, PA: Banner
   of Truth, 1986), 376–436, 472–78. Robinson, seeking refuge in Canada during the Civil
   War, preached several Sunday evening discourses, collected as *Slavery as Recognized in
   the Mosaic Civil Law, and as Recognized Also, and Allowed, in the Abrahamic, Mosaic, and*

of the church, preferring a more moderate and nuanced employ-
ment of the doctrine, more willing, in the end, to criticize slavery
than some of his fellow Old School Presbyterian brethren. Neither
Hodge nor his fellow Presbyterians, however, escaped the profound
and pervasive influence of slavery. The ways in which Presbyterians
interacted with slavery, defending it or opposing it, became a major
preoccupation for the church in the 1830s and later, especially for
the development of the doctrine of the spirituality of the church.

American Slavery

As representative of many in Northern Old School Presbyterianism, Hodge believed that a blanket condemnation of slavery, as
regularly issued by the abolitionists, was wrong since the Bible
did not condemn slavery as such but only its abuses. The Old
Testament regulated slavery by requiring Israelites to manumit
their countrymen after six years but permitted those in Israel to
enslave foreigners for life. From this biblical history, Hodge drew
the conclusion that it was not wrong in itself to enslave, though he
hoped and believed that general societal conditions over time would
render the plight of slaves in America better and emancipation
inevitable. Additionally, Hodge reasoned, Christ and his apostles
did not call for the abolition of slavery but regulated it with respect
to both slaves and masters.[3] Thus, Hodge argued, the tactics of the

---

Christian Church (Toronto: Rollo & Adam, 1865). Thornwell and Robinson defended
the institution of slavery and, in the name of the spirituality of the church, opposed those
who found the American expression of it unbiblical. These men were prepared to use the
pulpit to defend slavery and to attack those who called for its extirpation as violating the
spirituality of the church. To be sure, they called for reform of the institution, but they
otherwise wanted the church to be mute about slavery unless it was defending slavery and
calling masters and slaves to their duties.

3   Charles Hodge, review of *Slavery*, by William E. Channing, *BRTR* 8, no. 2 (1836): 274–79.

abolitionists tended to undermine the authority of Scripture since they proclaimed as one of the worst of evils that which Christ had not called evil at all.

Over time, particularly by the 1850s, it was not uncommon for abolitionists confronted with arguments showing that slavery itself was not forbidden by the Bible to see this as evidence of the Bible's insufficiency or unreliability. For instance, William Lloyd Garrison, publisher of the well-known abolitionist newspaper *The Liberator*, in 1845 "paid homage . . . to Thomas Paine for providing him with intellectual resources for getting beyond the Bible."[4] Garrison, who was earlier convinced of abolitionism by a Presbyterian arguing that it was unbiblical, ultimately came to believe that the passages of the Bible that supported (or at least seemed to support) slavery could simply be dismissed because one no longer needed to treat the Bible as infallible and could, in fact, see its errors at a number of points.

Mark Noll observes that

> Garrison's . . . willingness to jettison the Bible if the Bible was construed as legitimating slavery was too radical for most of his fellow Americans. In fact, the willingness of Garrison and a few others to favor abolitionism *in place of* Scripture actually worked to the advantage of those who defended slavery on the basis of Scripture.[5]

---

4 Mark A. Noll, *The Civil War as a Theological Crisis* (Chapel Hill: University of North Carolina Press, 2006), 31.

5 Noll, *Theological Crisis*, 32 (emphasis original). Americans largely remained wedded to the view that the Bible was infallible, not succumbing to Enlightenment "higher critical" views until the next century and so were not generally amenable to abolitionists who attacked Scripture. Many abolitionists made it clear that they had no greater concern than ending slavery, and if the Bible had to be pushed aside in the process, they were willing, and sometimes even happy, to do so.

As the tension between North and South heightened, biblical defenders of slavery came either to view or to characterize attacks on slavery as attacks on the Bible because to many Bible believers, like Hodge, it seemed patent that the Bible did not condemn slavery as a sin. Noll concludes,

> In short, the radicalism of all-out abolitionists like Garrison made it much harder for anyone who wanted to deploy the Bible in order to attack American slavery. Garrison's stance was more important for how it alienated those who continued to trust in the Bible than it was for attracting sympathizers.[6]

This is part of the reason that Hodge opposed abolitionism: its Bible-denying tactics only tended to strengthen the proslavery movement and militate against all calls for reform, gradual emancipation, and other more moderate measures.

We ought to step back and examine the deeper roots of American slavery and the Presbyterian Church's response to it. Many Englishmen came to Virginia as indentured servants: the perceived colony-wide need for slaves did not develop until late in the seventeenth century, particularly as labor-intensive crops became more widespread and certain prominent men increased their landholdings and looked for cheap labor to work their lands. While Northerners, like Hodge, did employ slaves,[7] even into the nineteenth century, chiefly as house or personal servants, the development of a more industrial economy in the North did not necessitate the large number of slaves working in the field as did the labor-intensive

6 Noll, *Theological Crisis*, 32.
7 For a discussion of Hodge's personal involvement with slavery, see Strange, *Spirituality of the Church*, chap. 2.

agricultural economy of the South. The South's economy developed over time, and slaves were used first in tobacco production and then in the growing and harvesting of rice, indigo, and, chiefly, cotton.[8]

Though the number of slaves grew during the seventeenth and eighteenth centuries, it seemed to many, as it did to some of the nation's founding fathers, that the institution of slavery was waning—or at least that it should be. Given the War for Independence, some believed that the freedom won by the English colonists would surely come soon to the slaves. Even then, the irony of American freedom being built on the back of American slavery, as noted later by certain American historians, was not lost on some at the time.[9] Though the US Constitution made certain provisions with respect to slavery, the word *slavery* appears nowhere in the document, and it was the apparent hope of more than a few of its drafters that after the ending of the transatlantic slave trade in 1808, the institution would shrivel.[10]

A new lease on life, however, came to slavery, at least in part, through the invention of the cotton gin. In 1793, Eli Whitney invented a machine that would efficiently and orderly separate the cotton seeds from the fiber without damage. Previously, it had taken enormous manpower simply to produce one pound of cotton, separating the seeds and fiber by hand. Now with Whitney's invention, cotton production became cost-effective, and the cotton industry, hitherto quite limited in the South, took off, especially after the

8   One of the best treatments of slavery in America remains Kenneth M. Stampp, *The Peculiar Institution: Slavery in the Ante-bellum South* (New York: Knopf, 1956).

9   This irony is the theme of the brilliant book by Edmund S. Morgan, *American Slavery, American Freedom* (New York: Norton, 1975).

10   The Constitution provided for the end of the slave trade in article 1, section 9, clause 1. An excellent discussion of the changing face of slavery in the early national period is found in Gordon S. Wood, *Empire of Liberty: A History of the Early Republic, 1789–1815*, Oxford History of the United States (New York: Oxford University Press, 2009), 508–42.

War of 1812. With slave traders seeking to import as many slaves as possible before the 1808 deadline, slavery was not declining but thriving.[11] Many regretted the ending of the slave trade and in the years thereafter smuggled in slaves: this, in addition to the growth of slave families, led to a burgeoning slave population. By the time of the US Civil War, the slave population in the South was about four million (the White population in the same region was about seven million).[12] The question whether slavery was waxing and would have continued indefinitely had not the Civil War abruptly ended it or whether it was waning and would have ended of its own accord has been hotly debated. In my view, a good case can be made that when the war came in 1861, slavery was, lamentably, a profitable, spreading institution with no end in sight.[13]

The Presbyterian Church's General Assembly of 1818

In 1818, the Presbyterian Church's General Assembly upheld the deposing of abolitionist George Bourne, who insisted that slave-

---

11 Picking up where Gordon Wood left off, Daniel Walker Howe has written arguably the definitive history of the years from the close of the War of 1812 to the close of the Mexican-American War and its aftermath (1815–1848). So much of the development of slavery and the changing attitudes toward it are chronicled in this book: *What Hath God Wrought: The Transformation of America, 1815–1848*, Oxford History of the United States (New York: Oxford University Press, 2007), 125–63 passim.

12 Robert William Fogel and Stanley L. Engerman's *Time on the Cross: The Economics of American Negro Slavery* (New York: Little, Brown, 1974) shocked scholarly sensibilities with its then-controversial claim that slavery was not crumbling under its own weight but was prospering and thriving, leading to the conclusion that gradual emancipation would not have worked and that abolition was warranted. This also means that the Civil War was, arguably, necessary to end slavery.

13 Lacy K. Ford, *Deliver Us from Evil: The Slavery Question in the Old South* (New York: Oxford University Press, 2009), is an excellent treatment of all the complexities involved in the typically oversimplified account of the development of "the acceptance of slavery as a necessary evil in the early republic to the embrace of the institution as a positive good in the late antebellum period" (5).

holders receive church discipline.[14] In the aftermath of the case, that same assembly, perhaps to make itself clear on the principle, adopted a remarkable and somewhat surprising statement condemning slavery.[15] The statement begins as follows:

> We consider the voluntary enslaving of one part of the human race by another, as a gross violation of the most precious and sacred rights of human nature; as utterly inconsistent with the law of God, which requires us to love our neighbor as ourselves, and as totally irreconcilable with the spirit and principles of the gospel of Christ. . . . It is manifestly the duty of all Christians who enjoy the light of the present day, when the inconsistency of slavery, both with the dictates of humanity and religion, has been demonstrated, and is generally seen and acknowledged, to use their honest, earnest, and unwearied endeavours, to correct the errors of former times, and as speedily as possible to efface this blot on our holy religion, and to obtain the complete abolition of slavery throughout Christendom, and if possible throughout the world.[16]

Hodge heartily approved this statement criticizing slavery and calling for its extirpation in America. Decades later, when this

---

14 See Strange, *Spirituality of the Church*, 185–89, and the excellent book by Ryan C. Mc-Ilhenny, *To Preach Deliverance to the Captives: Freedom and Slavery in the Protestant Mind of George Bourne, 1780–1845* (Baton Rouge: Louisiana State University Press, 2020).

15 Some historians have suggested that collective guilt over deposing a man defending the truth moved the 1818 General Assembly also to adopt such a strong condemnation of slavery as it did in its 1818 statement.

16 Samuel J. Baird, *A Collection of the Acts, Deliverances, and Testimonies of the Supreme Judicatory of the Presbyterian Church* (Philadelphia: Presbyterian Board of Publications, 1855), 820–21. Baird is cited here (instead of the 1818 minutes merely) because he collects in one place all the General Assembly actions having to do with slavery. The 1818 statement is a breath of fresh air amid all the statements; had its counsel been heeded and slavery abolished, one can only wonder at the difference that would have made in the United States.

statement seemed to have fallen into disuse, Hodge remembered that the General Assembly had expressed such noble sentiment in 1818 and that it had not in the following years repealed it.[17] Remarkably, this statement was adopted without dissent. Much happened, however, between the issuing of this historic condemnation of slavery and Hodge's first article critiquing slavery in 1836. In part, the kind of immediate abolitionism advocated by Bourne, including a call for the excommunication of slave owners, took root in places other than the Presbyterian Church and began to grow particularly in the 1830s. Further, not only did Nat Turner's slave revolt terrify the South, but more generally, the press fostered the specter of slaves rising in the night to kill their masters, and the South professed to be besieged by the abolitionists and those who wanted to destroy their "way of life."[18] The clarion call of the 1818 General Assembly is a curious thing: soon after it was made, the consensus unraveled within the church, North and South, that slavery was at best a necessary evil and ought to be brought to an end, and it became increasingly difficult in the South to oppose slavery openly.

17 Charles Hodge, "General Assembly," *BRPR* 18, no. 3 (1846): 420–28. In his General Assembly report, Hodge, who was moderator in 1846, made it clear that he believed the assembly was consistent in its declarations on slavery and that there was harmony between the 1818 General Assembly and others that followed—especially the 1845 General Assembly, which held that slavery in itself is not sinful.

18 For an excellent account of the Nat Turner revolt of 1831 in Virginia (and the earlier Denmark Vesey scare, in South Carolina in 1822), see Ford, *Deliver Us from Evil*, 207–37, 338–60. Though the Vesey uprising did not materialize, the Turner revolt resulted in the death of about fifty Whites, terrifying Whites (and resulting in a brutal retaliation against Blacks, slave and free). Also, Charles F. Irons observes that following the Nat Turner revolt, "white evangelicals . . . never did rebuild the same level of trust, cooperation in ministry, or interracial fellowship that had existed in the 1820s." Irons, *The Origins of Proslavery Christianity: White and Black Evangelicals in Colonial and Antebellum Virginia* (Chapel Hill: University of North Carolina Press, 2008), 134.

The Changing Scene of Slavery

As a part of the changing scene, positions on both sides hardened. The South went from a mild defense of slavery, even a "necessary evil" defense in some cases, to a position that slavery was a positive good, an institution not meant to fade away. In the old view, many Southerners even admitted that the founding fathers had thought that slavery would fall under its own weight. According to the new approach, however, slavery was here to stay, increase, spread, and flourish.[19] While some may have articulated overtly biblical defenses of slavery much earlier,[20] one of the first to adopt this more militant defense of slavery, certainly in the 1830s, was the first Presbyterian minister in Mississippi, James Smylie.

Smylie preached that the Scriptures, contrary to popular belief, did not condemn slavery but approved it. Such teaching was a novelty at the time. Upon an initial hearing, fellow ministers urged him never to preach that again. As Peter Wallace notes, "While others had shown that Scripture did not consider slaveholding a sin, few had argued from Scripture that slavery was a positive good that should continue indefinitely."[21] Smylie likened the institution of slavery to the institution of marriage, arguing that both called for a certain sort of submission

19 As seen in Hodge, "General Assembly" (1846): 425. Hodge had no patience for something "so monstrous [and] in such obvious conflict with the principles of the Word of God" as those who believed that "slavery is a good and perpetual institution and ought to be perpetuated" (424).

20 Jewel L. Spangler, "Proslavery Presbyterians: Virginia's Conservative Dissenters in the Age of Revolution," *JPH* 78, no. 2 (2000): 111–23. Also, for the surprising New England roots of the defense of slavery, see Larry Tise, *A History of the Defense of Slavery in America, 1701–1840* (Athens: University of Georgia Press, 1990). And for the continuation of such, see Drew Gilpin Faust, ed., *The Ideology of Slavery: Proslavery Thought in the Antebellum South, 1830–1860* (Baton Rouge: Louisiana State University Press, 1981).

21 Peter J. Wallace, " 'The Bond of Union': The Old School Presbyterian Church and the American Nation, 1837–1861" (PhD diss., University of Notre Dame, 2004), 39–40. My treatment of Smylie relies on Wallace's unpublished dissertation.

and that both had potential for abuses: even as parents might abuse their power, so might slave owners abuse theirs. The answer was for slaveholders and slaves to do their biblical duties with respect to each other, not to eliminate the institution of slavery. Though Smylie's argument initially was met with revulsion, over the course of the 1840s and 1850s, his position gradually became the dominant one in a South that was set for a vigorous defense of the "peculiar institution."

Soon such a defense was taken up by statesmen, most notably the Southerner in the great senatorial triumvirate of the nineteenth century, John C. Calhoun of South Carolina.[22] The author of nullification and ardent defender of state sovereignty, Calhoun argued that slavery was part of the glory of the South and that it permitted a whole class of men to pursue the finer and nobler things of life. He argued that it was for the benefit of the slave and the master and that it was not contrary to biblical and natural law, as many argued, but was in fact in keeping with natural law.[23] This line of argument found its high-water mark in the infamous speech of Alexander Stephens, vice president of the Confederacy, in which Stephens argued that slavery was indeed the "cornerstone" of a free and prosperous (White) society.[24]

22 The other two members of this troika were Henry Clay and Daniel Webster. Though Calhoun has long been viewed as retrograde—archdefender of slavery that he was—his political philosophy, apart from this giant flaw, has been rediscovered and his genius appreciated. This is seen especially in a work like that of Guy Story Brown, *Calhoun's Philosophy of Politics: A Study of "A Disquisition on Government"* (Macon, GA: Mercer University Press, 2000).

23 Calhoun was the leading exponent of the doctrine of the "positive good" of slavery. Howe, *What Hath God Wrought*, 480. The effect of this notion in the following period may be seen in the seminal work by David M. Potter, *The Impending Crisis, 1848–1861* (New York: Harper and Row, 1976). It is interesting that many today who make a natural-law argument against slavery assume that it is patent; in fact, it was not uncommon, following Calhoun, for Southern statesmen in the mid-nineteenth century to argue *for* slavery using a natural-law argument.

24 Repudiating the vision of the founding fathers (that slavery was at the time a necessary evil that would surely, if gradually, wither away), Stephens argued in his famous address

The rising temperature of the rhetoric troubled Hodge, and he thought that as both sides radicalized, the debate between them simply yielded more heat than light.[25] He particularly believed, not without justification, that the abolition movement was galvanizing a reaction among slaveholders—an all-out defense of slavery on their part, different from before—prompting them to abandon all commitments to improve the slaves' condition, thus postponing, perhaps indefinitely, their ultimate emancipation.[26] In the meantime, Hodge always sought a moderating position because he wanted to maintain the union of the church and the union of the nation. In fact, because he saw the unity of the church *as* the bond of the nation, he appears to have been willing to bend over further than he otherwise might have been, in hopes of maintaining ecclesiastical union—and thus civil union. Hodge believed that the rhetoric and tone of the General Assembly deliverance of 1818 was appropriate and that if that moderate, even tone could be kept, Southern men would be more likely to listen, to come around, to educate their slaves, and to prepare them for freedom.[27] There is

in Savannah, Georgia, in the spring of 1861, that slavery is the foundation of a truly free society and that the new Confederacy's "cornerstone rests upon the great truth that the negro is not equal to the white man; that slavery . . . is his natural and normal condition." James McPherson, *Battle Cry of Freedom: The Civil War Era*, Oxford History of the United States (New York: Oxford University Press, 2003), 244. Hodge completely repudiated this idea as seen above and in his view of the unity of the human race.

25 Hodge wrote, "It is not by argument that the abolitionists have produced the present unhappy excitement. Argument has not been the characteristic of their publications. Denunciations of [the strongest sort of slavery and slaveholders] have formed the stapel [*sic*] of their addresses to the public." Hodge, review of *Slavery*, 270.

26 Hodge noted, "Abolitionists . . . have produced a state of alarming exasperation at the south, injurious to the slave and dangerous to the country, while they have failed to enlist the feelings of the north." Hodge, review of *Slavery*, 271. All this, Hodge reasoned, resulted in the strengthening rather than the diminishing of the institution of slavery.

27 This is the burden of all the articles that Hodge wrote in the *BRPR* with respect to slavery before the Civil War and emancipation.

no evidence, however, that anything like this had gone on or was going on in society at large or even in the church in particular.[28]

Both abolitionists like Bourne, at the time, and scholars, in following years, have wondered whether the 1818 statement on slavery was merely lip service to earlier Presbyterian commitments to end slavery, perhaps even a ruse to becalm emancipationists and salve consciences rightly smitten with a sense of the iniquity of American slavery. Many antislavery proponents suspected that the 1818 statement, while intending to do nothing but engage in an indefinite postponement of the question, was a ploy with no real end in sight, permitting inaction with respect to ending, or even contemplating ending, the debilitating institution.[29] The truth is that once slavery became profitable, and it clearly had by the 1830s, its defenders and proponents increased and had no apparent intention of seeing it end.[30]

The 1818 call of the General Assembly was a voice crying in the wilderness, unheeded by Presbyterian slave owners, who, together

28 This was James Patterson's complaint in his critique of the 1845 General Assembly, as seen in Strange, *Spirituality of the Church*, 203–7.

29 In a number of things that George Bourne wrote after his deposition in Virginia in 1817, he complained that the 1818 General Assembly declaration against slavery was a paper tiger, serving only as a cover for slaveholders, who should be excommunicated, he continued to maintain, for continuing in their sin. On this topic, see especially his *Man-Stealing and Slavery Denounced by the Presbyterian and Methodist Churches, Together with an Address to All the Churches* (Boston: Garrison & Knapp, 1834).

30 In fact, the South became so strident and unified in the defense of slavery that dissent was rare and, increasingly, dangerous (unlike in the North, where abolitionism was frequently criticized, and slavery in general debated, as seen in the case of Hodge and many others). For works that treat Southern dissent broadly, see Georgia Lee Tatum, *Disloyalty in the Confederacy* (1934; repr., Whitefish, MT: Literary Licensing, 2011); Carl N. Degler, *The Other South: Southern Dissenters in the Nineteenth Century* (New York: Harper and Row, 1974). For a work that treats dissent specifically in its clerical forms, see David B. Chesebrough, *Clergy Dissent in the Old South, 1830–1865* (Carbondale: Southern Illinois University Press, 1996).

with other slave owners, were not engaged in the betterment of conditions ("improvements") for their slaves, readying them for emancipation. Perhaps they were improving the slaves in anticipation of selling them, or they were thinking of ways to improve their own fortunes. But there is no evidence whatsoever that the ecclesiastical calls of the nineteenth century for slave betterment in anticipation of emancipation were ever heeded. The acquisition of Western states (especially Texas in 1845), the Mexican-American War (1846–1848), and many of the legislative and judicial acts pertaining to slavery in the decade leading up to the Civil War, starting with the Compromise of 1850 and its Fugitive Slave Act, including the horrific Dred Scott decision of 1857, gave ever-renewed hope to slave owners that theirs was a thriving and flourishing institution and that secession was warranted to preserve what slave owners saw as a glorious way of life.[31]

Hodge's position in his 1836 essay was not, as was misrepresented (particularly later), that slavery was unproblematic.[32] While he held that the Bible did not condemn the slaveholder as a sinner worthy of excommunication, he did insist that Christ and his apostles,

31 Even when calling for secession, no small part of the argument was the profitability and usefulness of slavery, made more so by the events of the 1840s and 1850s. For one of the most chilling and persuasive accounts of the real reason for secession, a resolute determination to preserve slavery and promote White supremacy, see Charles B. Dew, *Apostles of Disunion: Southern Secession Commissioners and the Causes of the Civil War* (Charlottesville: University of Virginia Press, 2002).

32 Hodge's 1836 essay and his 1851 essay supporting the fugitive slave laws (to uphold the Compromise of 1850) were both published, together with a number of proslavery essays, at the time of the Civil War, with Hodge's essays being edited, apparently without his knowledge, to make it appear only that he supported slavery, not that he also harshly criticized its practices, as found particularly at the end of his 1836 essay. Hodge, "The Bible Argument on Slavery," in *Cotton Is King, and Pro-Slavery Arguments: Comprising the Writings of Hammond, Harper, Christy, Stringfellow, Hodge, Bledsoe, and Cartwright, on This Important Subject*, ed. E. N. Elliott (Augusta, GA: Pritchard, Abbott & Loomis, 1860), 841–77; Hodge, "The Fugitive Slave Law," in Elliott, *Cotton Is King*, 809–40.

together with the Old Testament, regulated slavery. He took a good deal of time making an abstract defense of slavery ipso facto, though he excoriated abolitionists for dealing in abstractions.[33] Only late in the 1836 article did Hodge clearly reveal his real goal concerning slavery (in addition to his earlier enunciated goal of "improvement"). He wrote that he had "another motive in the preparation of this article" than simply to defend slavery as it existed in the United States.[34] Insofar as the abolitionists continually focused the discussion on the abstract wrongness of all slavery, the slaveholder concentrated on defending the institution and was "withdrawn from far more important points[, namely,] the manner in which he treats his slaves and the laws enacted for the security of his possession. These are the points on which his judgment might be much more readily convicted of error, and his conscience of sin."[35]

Hodge proceeded with emancipationist arguments, contending that the slave was due just compensation for his labor, which included more than merely providing him with food, clothing, and shelter. He ought to have an opportunity to purchase his freedom and in a whole host of ways to improve himself. All masters ought to afford such for their slaves, and laws should be amended to accomplish these things. Hodge went further in this than many others who disliked slavery at the time did: "It may be objected," he wrote, "that if the slaves are allowed so to improve as to become freemen, the next step in their progress is that they should become citizens."[36] Perhaps surprisingly, Hodge conceded,

33 Hodge, review of *Slavery*, 292.
34 Hodge, review of *Slavery*, 298.
35 Hodge, review of *Slavery*, 299.
36 Hodge, review of *Slavery*, 304–5.

We admit this is so. . . . This is the natural progress of society, and it should be allowed this freely to expand itself, or it will work its own destruction. . . . This objection would not be considered of any force, if the slaves in this country were not of a different race from their masters.[37]

Hodge hit the problem squarely on the head: slavery in America and the question of freedom for the slaves was all tied up with the question of race. "Still," Hodge reminded his readers, "they [the slaves] are men; their colour does not place them beyond the operation of the principles of the gospel, or from under the protection of God." Hodge admitted, candidly, his (lamentable) view of these things in a footnote, holding that because "the master and slave belong to different races, [this] precludes the possibility of their living together on equal terms." At the same time, Hodge argued, it is not the case that "the one has a right to oppress the other."[38] The solution, as Hodge saw it, is that they should separate. Hence Hodge and many other "enlightened" people of his era supported African colonization.[39]

Hodge ended his first work on slavery by admonishing both sides: "Let then the North remember that they are bound to follow

---

37 Hodge, review of *Slavery*, 305.

38 Hodge, review of *Slavery*, 305.

39 The American Colonization Society was founded in Princeton, New Jersey, in 1816 (with Hodge's elder colleagues Archibald Alexander and Samuel Miller among the founders) and had among its many supporters Henry Clay, Abraham Lincoln, and Charles Hodge. The purpose of the society was to see African slaves emancipated and returned to Africa: the colony of Liberia was planted in 1821 for this purpose. The reasons for this desire that free Blacks leave the United States were mixed: some members of the society feared "amalgamation" (racial intermarriage) and Black-White socialization above all, while others, more humanely, simply feared that former African slaves would never be permitted to earn the respect necessary to live as equals among Whites in America (certainly Lincoln's sentiments). For a helpful work on the subject, see Eric Burin, *Slavery and the Peculiar Solution: A History of the American Colonization Society* (Gainesville: University of Florida Press, 2005).

the example of Christ in the manner of treating slavery, and the South that they are bound to follow the precepts of Christ in their manner of treating their slaves."[40] A right understanding of the power and province of the church—of the spirituality of the church—meant, for Hodge, that the church ought not to go beyond the word of God: slavery, as Hodge then reckoned it, was not sinful, but slaves should be treated as those made in the image of God.

A Case against Slavery by Those Who Pioneered Spirituality Arguments

A stronger case than Hodge's against slavery (and the deliverances of the 1845 General Assembly, which Hodge defended but many lamented as too accommodating to slavery)[41] was made by some in the 1840s, from both Scotland and the United States.[42] Another case against slavery in America was made by Reformed Presbyterians in the States, heirs of the Scottish Covenanters, who had pioneered many of the arguments for the spirituality, or the spiritual independence, of the church.[43] Alexander McLeod, pastor of the Reformed Presbyterian Congregation in New York City, had, at the beginning of the century, engaged almost all the questions that Hodge and others eventually did with respect to slavery.[44] McLeod saw slavery,

40 Hodge, review of *Slavery*, 305.
41 Strange, *Spirituality of the Church*, 196–202. The 1845 General Assembly invoked a form of the spirituality of the church in the name of preserving church union for the sake of the American Union, especially in light of the divisions of the Baptists and Methodists in the previous two years.
42 Strange, *Spirituality of the Church*, 203–7.
43 Strange, *Spirituality of the Church*, 207–11.
44 Alexander McLeod, *Negro Slavery Unjustifiable: A Discourse* (New York: T. & J. Swords, 1802). The Covenanters and their heirs in America have an ancient and honorable record of opposing slavery, refusing to allow any of their members to be slaveholders.

as did Bourne and others, as manstealing, a violation of Exodus 21:16; 1 Timothy 1:10; and other biblical passages.

Men, women, and children had been plucked from Africa, either by other tribes that warred to sell to slavers or by direct sale to slavers, and brought to the New World involuntarily and inhumanely. McLeod made all the standard antislavery arguments but also skillfully answered the main objections brought against emancipation, more coolheadedly than later antislavery proponents tended to do. One of the weaknesses, in fact, of many Christian antislavery advocates was that they asserted, rightly, general biblical principles of love of neighbor but failed to answer the biblical passages that seemed to recognize and permit slavery. McLeod asserted love of neighbor and dealt with the difficult Bible passages concerning slavery.

The first two objections that McLeod sought to answer were not biblical but cultural and anthropological: the first, that Europeans are superior to Africans, and the second, that Blacks form an inferior race to Whites. Hodge, it should be noted, always argued for the unity of humankind and would not permit Africans to be represented as anything other than fully human.[45]

The third objection was biblical: Blacks are the descendants of Ham and under a curse.[46] McLeod responded in several ways to

45 David Torbett has argued, convincingly, that Hodge affirmed the unity of the race (White and Black are "one blood" and both "in the image of God") and thus was less racist and more hopeful about the possibility of future racial harmony than "progressives" (like Horace Bushnell), who saw only a troubled future for the races in their seeking to live together, arguing that burgeoning Darwinism supported White supremacy. See Torbett, *Theology and Slavery: Charles Hodge and Horace Bushnell* (Macon, GA: Mercer University Press, 2006). See also from Hodge, "The Unity of Mankind," *BRPR* 31, no. 1 (1859): 103–49; "Diversity of Species in the Human Race," *BRPR* 34, no. 3 (1862): 453–64.

46 Gen. 9 records that after disembarking, Noah planted a vineyard, produced wine, became drunk, and in some fashion debauched himself. Ham discovered him naked in his tent, and rather than covering him, as his two brothers did, Ham mocked him. Noah cursed his son Canaan in response. Noah's three sons—Ham, Shem, and Japheth—became the fathers

this claim, chiefly by pointing out that it was Canaan, not Ham, who received the curse and that in redemptive history "this prediction has had its accomplishment three thousand years ago. The descendants of Shem did, by divine direction, under the conduct of Joshua, subjugate the offspring of Canaan, when they took possession of the promised land."[47]

The fourth objection was related to the third: "God permitted the ancient Israelites to hold their fellow creatures in servitude." McLeod admitted that this was the case and looked at the two major instances in which this occurred. The first concerned their fellow Israelites, and the second concerned strangers, those of Canaan and the surrounding nations. First, the instances in which a Hebrew might reduce a fellow Hebrew to servitude (though never for his whole life) were "theft and insolvency." In either case, it was when the thief or debtor could in no other way repay, and the term of service was never more than six years. It was the kind of involuntary servitude that continues for someone judged guilty of a crime. Second, reducing the stranger to lifelong servitude, like the fulfillment of the Ham/Canaan curse, also had to do with redemptive history. According to the Old Testament, God gave to Israel, as his chosen nation, the unique calling to dispossess the Canaanite nations and to inhabit the land in their place. When one of those

of Africans, Asians, and Europeans, respectively, or so some argued. There is a significant literature that treats how, in the late medieval and early modern period in the West, it became common to regard the "curse of Ham" as justifying the enslavement of Africans, who are assumed to have been Ham or Canaan's descendants. A recent work dealing with this curious history is David M. Whitford, *The Curse of Ham in the Early Modern Era: The Bible and the Justifications for Slavery* (Burlington, VT: Ashgate, 2009).

47 McLeod, *Negro Slavery Unjustifiable*, 28. He hereby identified the Canaanites as those on whom the "curse of Ham" fell when Israel invaded and conquered what became its homeland. McLeod saw the "Ham curse" as having nothing to do with Africans, much less with justifying their enslavement in perpetuity.

nations, however, voluntarily submitted to Israel's governance, God's people might show mercy, and though "extermination was the command," upon their "voluntary subjection they were only reduced into a state of servitude"—and even then, the "Israelites were forbidden to use them harshly."[48]

McLeod's point was that Israel's enslaving of other nations was not an example for the Christian church to follow but was unique to her redemptive-historical situation. Hodge and other Old School Presbyterians had such arguments at their disposal. That they failed or refused to make recourse to such biblical-theological reasoning but simply repeated the tired nostrum "The Bible does not condemn slavery, and neither can we" testifies not to the spirituality of the church but to the cultural captivity of the church. Hodge's position, as we will see, developed beyond the 1845 General Assembly, showing itself as more nuanced and supple as the years passed, yet still falling short of what was needed: the kind of candor that McLeod evinced in denouncing American slavery as an evil not to be tolerated but to be eliminated.

The fifth objection dealt with the New Testament attitude toward slavery even as the fourth dealt with the Old Testament position on it. Here is how McLeod pointedly expressed the common objection that the New Testament did not proscribe slavery: "Slavery was tolerated, in the primitive ages of Christianity, by the Roman laws. It is not condemned by Christ or his Apostles. They have given directions for the conduct of master and slave, I Tim. vi.1. They have not intimated that the keeping of men in slavery was sinful." This anticipates rather accurately the kind of

---

48 McLeod, *Negro Slavery Unjustifiable*, 31. The Gibeonites serve as an example of people reduced to permanent servitude, whom Israel, had she not been deceived, would otherwise have eliminated in her conquest of the land.

defense that Hodge and the 1845 General Assembly gave for why slavery as such is not sinful. McLeod responded first by affirming that because of 1 Timothy 1:10 (forbidding manstealing), the New Testament does, in fact, prohibit slavery. Other passages, like Colossians 4:1, that command masters to give servants "that which is just and equal" (McLeod's paraphrase) require something that in no measure corresponded to the reality or practice of American slavery: they require that masters "treat [their slaves] justly; use them mercifully; pay them lawful wages; give them an equivalent for their services."[49] The practice of American slavery was opposed to these injunctions entirely and would never have functioned as it did under such strictures.

McLeod argued that if one takes the position that the New Testament's silence on the abuses of the Greek and Roman slavery of the time means that the New Testament is unconcerned with abusive slavery in the classical era, that argument proves too much. If the New Testament's silence to the horrors of classical slavery (as we've seen earlier in this chapter) means that Christians were justified in being slaveholders and were abjectly to submit as slaves, then "it will prove the justice of the worst of tyranny, the most dreadful cruelty, because Nero is not specified as an infamous tyrant in the New Testament."[50] If the failure of the New Testament to condemn every horror of Roman slavery means that such slavery is permissible, "it will prove that you have a right to sell your own children as slaves—to kidnap your neighbour, your countryman, and your friend. You need not, therefore, confine your traffic in human flesh to the African race."[51]

---

49 McLeod, *Negro Slavery Unjustifiable*, 33.

50 McLeod, *Negro Slavery Unjustifiable*, 34.

51 McLeod, *Negro Slavery Unjustifiable*, 34. The Romans practiced all these cited abuses, and neither Christ nor his apostles denounced such vile practices. Surely, McLeod reasoned, such a lack of denunciation does not mean that Christ approved of such vile behavior.

To suggest to any White American of the time that the acceptability of slavery meant the permissibility of Whites being enslaved was unthinkable. For Americans, the only acceptable slavery was Black slavery, a conviction that by itself demonstrates how contemptible and wrong the institution of chattel slavery in America was.

Therefore, it argues too much to keep affirming, as most in the Old School did, that since Christ did not denounce slavery, it must mean that he approved of it. McLeod mentions one further abuse and then ends his sermon with a several-page plea to have mercy on the poor, oppressed Africans.

3

The Spirituality of the Church
Preceding the US Civil War

AS SECTIONAL CONFLICT in the United States increased throughout the 1840s and 1850s, politics became more dominant in every
sphere, threatening to overshadow all concerns. Old School Presbyterians of all stripes affirmed in these pre–Civil War years that the
church had a particular province in which it ought to remain but
disagreed on how exactly Scripture would have the church carry
that out. Some saw the spirituality of the church acting as a kind
of regulative principle of church government, tightly restricting the
church's proper focus, while others saw the spirituality of the church
as broader and looser in its conception.[1] What was the relationship
of the church to slavery? To whom was political allegiance due in
the Civil War (Union or Confederacy)? Did the Bible set forth a
detailed church government? These questions are explored below.[2]

---

1 Alan D. Strange, "Commentary on the Form of Government of the Orthodox Presbyterian
   Church," *Ordained Servant Online* (April 2020): 34–35, https://www.opc.org/os.html.
2 And they are discussed more fully in Strange, *Spirituality of the Church*.

Prelude to the 1861 General Assembly

The doctrine of the spirituality of the church, however hitherto shaped by reactions to slavery, took on a different dimension at the General Assembly of 1861, especially in the polity of Charles Hodge. Before that momentous 1861 assembly, at the 1859 General Assembly, when James Henley Thornwell had called for discussing the spirituality of the church, Hodge was dubious about Thornwell's version of it, which seemed to Hodge calculated to justify the church in dodging any issue that she preferred to avoid. And then at the 1860 General Assembly, the spirituality of the church arose once again in the debates of Hodge and Thornwell, this time on the broader question of the boards that governed church ministries like home and foreign missions and church education and publications, as well as questions pertaining to the nature of Presbyterianism, the nature and limits of church power, and the province of the church with respect to the state.[3] In the aftermath of the discussions and debates of the 1860 General Assembly, Hodge remained unconvinced that the doctrine of the spirituality of the church as set forth by Thornwell and his allies was viable or helpful.

These last elements—particularly church and state questions—remained at the fore as the General Assembly commenced in 1861, but they had an entirely different feel about them. There was a new urgency, a crisis atmosphere, at the 1861 General Assembly because of what had happened in civil society between the assembly of 1860 and that of 1861. Abraham Lincoln was elected president of the United States in November 1860. Because Lincoln had campaigned and been elected on a platform opposing all extension of slavery

3 Strange, *Spirituality of the Church*, 228–37. See also Alan D. Strange, "Charles Hodge on Office and the Nature of Presbyterianism," in *Charles Hodge: American Orthodox Reformed Theologian*, ed. Ryan M. McGraw (Leiden: Vandenhoeck and Ruprecht, 2023), 231–66.

into the territories, having the effect of limiting slavery to where it existed and preventing its spread, the Southern states, in none of which Lincoln had been on the ballot, began to secede—that is, to withdraw from the Union to form their own confederacy.[4]

These developments, particularly secession and the specter of war, were distressing to Old School Presbyterians, to Thornwell no less than Hodge. Thornwell was a "Union" man, as were all the leading Old School Presbyterians of the South. Thornwell, having returned from Europe in 1860, proposed the emancipation of the slaves in order to save the Union.[5] But with the successive withdrawal of Southern states from the Union, beginning with Thornwell's state of South Carolina in December 1860 (and ten others seceding in the following days and months), hopes for the continuance of an intact United States dimmed. Over against such an eventuality, Hodge published "The State of the Country" in the January 1861 issue of the *Biblical Repertory and Princeton Review* and "The Church and Country" in the April issue of the same year. Clearly, all thoughts were turned to the national crisis: how to save the Union (and induce seceded states to return) and to avert the horrors of war. Hodge's first article was written before South Carolina's secession, with Hodge making every argument he could as to why secession was not called for and would be a disaster.[6] In the second article,

---

4   On the rise of Lincoln and the violent reaction against it in the Southern states, see Sean Wilentz, *The Rise of American Democracy: Jefferson to Lincoln* (New York: Norton, 2005).

5   William W. Freehling, "James Henley Thornwell's Mysterious Antislavery Moment," *JSH* 57, no. 3 (1991): 383–406. Thornwell went with his state, South Carolina, when it seceded, but he was in favor of the Union historically and was even willing ultimately, as Freehling notes, to abolish slavery to save the Union.

6   While Robert J. Breckinridge agreed with and appreciated Hodge's January 1861 article, his comment about it was accurate: "Your article in the *Repertory* . . . will not . . . satisfy any except temperate and thoughtful persons." Breckinridge predicted disunion and war—Hodge and Lincoln underestimated the will and resolve of Southerners on this matter. Robert J.

secession had occurred, but Hodge wrote it before the outbreak of war with the Southern firing on Fort Sumter on April 12, 1861.[7]

In "The State of the Country," Hodge perceived some need to justify his foray into civil matters in a journal devoted largely to ecclesiastical matters. "There are occasions," Hodge wrote, "when political questions rise into the sphere of morals and religion; when the rule for political action is to be sought, not in considerations of state policy but in the law of God. On such occasions, the distinction between secular and religious journals is obliterated."[8] This was such an extraordinary occasion, as Hodge saw it, in which the threat of disunion imperiled the nation and the church in the nation. Hodge fervently believed that the United States was to serve as a city on a hill, a political and religious model to the rest of the world, a beacon of freedom and holiness that a civil war threatened to bring to an ignominious end. Though Hodge was highly political personally, he sought publicly to downplay partisanship, and it was indeed an extraordinary situation at hand, the dissolution of the nation, that Hodge believed warranted his address of civil affairs so directly in the pages of the *Biblical Repertory and Princeton Review*.

Breckinridge to Charles Hodge, 19 January 1861, box 28, folder 21, Charles Hodge Manuscript Collection (CHMC), Special Collections, Princeton Theological Seminary Library. In correspondence with Peter Walker, Hodge noted that "nine tenths" of the response to his January 1861 article was "greatly in its favour," while also admitting that he was "greatly harassed by some over the article." Hodge to Peter Walker, n.d., box 46, folder 30, CHMC. Hodge was especially upset that his good friend and Princeton Theological Seminary board president, Henry Boardman, who had seen an advance copy of the article, sent Hodge "a very serious remonstrance against the appearance of my article in the *Princeton Review*." Hodge to Peter Walker, 12 December 1860, box 46, folder 30, CHMC. See also Hodge to Peter Walker, 17 December 1860, box 46, folder 30, CHMC.

7   Hodge noted, with dismay, that some copies of the April 1861 article, after the outbreak of the war, "have been returned, as refused," the mail in the South being censored. Hodge to Peter Walker, 1 May 1861, folder 46, box 30, CHMC.

8   Charles Hodge, "The State of the Country," *BRPR* 33, no. 1 (1861): 1.

Hodge was seen throughout the church as a moderate, un-like the Southerners, who were seen as more extreme with their defense of slavery, or Robert J. Breckinridge, who was seen as a man who loved to fight altogether too much. Hodge expressed to his brother Hugh that he intended to maintain the peace by his article.[9] Indeed, many in the North were heartened by it, but his friends in the South attacked and rejected it.[10] And insofar as Hodge remained opposed in principle to abolitionism, the abolitionists of the North attacked it as still currying favor with the South and seeking yet to appease them so that they would remain in the Union.[11]

Though Hodge viewed the situation as an acute crisis meriting attention in a theological journal—and, as noted, others were to follow in the war years—he could still maintain that he had made no undue intrusion into matters that were more purely civil or political because he was neither preaching from the pulpit (having far more license in a journal article than in a sermon) nor urging the church as an institution to adopt his view. On any proper view of the spirituality of the church, Hodge had not, in his view, transgressed by addressing the more purely political in either of his

9   Charles Hodge to Hugh Hodge, 13 December 1860, box 12, folder 2, Charles Hodge Papers (CHP), Department of Rare Books and Special Collections, Princeton University Library.
10 Charles Hodge to Hugh Hodge, 18 February 1861, box 12, folder 2, CHP. This negative reception of his article by many in the South vexed Hodge greatly. One correspondent went so far as to say, in reference to Hodge's January 1861 article, that it would "denationalize the Seminary and confine it to the Northern States." John Miller to Charles Hodge, 7 January 1861, box 28, folder 20, CHMC. Hodge expressed dismay at the prominent churchman's conviction that Hodge's article would be ruinous for Hodge and the seminary. Hodge to Leighton Wilson, 3 January 1861, box 28, folder 20, CHMC.
11 Paul C. Gutjahr, *Charles Hodge: Guardian of American Orthodoxy* (New York: Oxford University Press, 2011), 311–17. Hodge's January 1861 article was followed by an article in the South from Thornwell, upholding his version of the spirituality of the church. Hodge's April 1861 article was, in part, a response to Thornwell.

two prewar articles, and he certainly hoped that the church would observe such strictures.[12]

Hodge's hopes for the church as an institution to maintain her proper spirituality and to avoid improper political pronouncements threatening the bonds of union of the Presbyterian Church, though the times were tempestuous, were thoroughly dashed at the 1861 General Assembly. As Hodge scholar John Stewart puts it, "In the history of American Presbyterianism, no General Assembly can equal the one that met in Philadelphia in May of 1861. For drama and long-range consequences, it is without peer. By the time the assembly adjourned, all the Southern states had withdrawn from the Union except Tennessee and North Carolina."[13] What precisely went on at the 1861 General Assembly bears telling in some detail because it particularly reveals where Hodge was regarding the spirituality of the church and the role that the doctrine played at that assembly.

The 1861 General Assembly

Since the war had already begun when the assembly convened in Philadelphia on May 16, 1861, commissioners from the Southern presbyteries and synods were either ill-represented or not represented at all.[14] The Synods of North Carolina, South Carolina, Geor-

---

12 While some correspondents excoriated Hodge for expressing what he did in the two articles as inappropriate for a clergyman, several correspondents (particularly as reflected in box 15, CHP) commended him, especially several letters from an L. Elmers (letters dated 15 and 21 January 1861 and 11 March 1861, box 15, folder 50, CHP), begging Hodge to use his influence to avert war, arguing that if Hodge called for letting the South go in peace, Hodge was so influential that "the course you take in this matter may decide the question."

13 John Stewart, "Charles Hodge as a Public Theologian," in *Theology as Conversation: The Significance of Dialogue in Historical and Contemporary Theology; A Festschrift for Daniel L. Migliore*, ed. Bruce L. McCormack and Kimlyn J. Bender (Grand Rapids, MI: Eerdmans, 2009), 350–51.

14 Though the meeting place of the General Assembly was chosen by the previous General Assembly, and the previous assembly (1860) had no way of knowing the events of 1861,

gia, Alabama, and Arkansas had no commissioners in attendance.[15] The Synod of Virginia had only one minister and one elder present, representing one presbytery (Greenbrier), which would become part of West Virginia.[16] The Synods of Memphis and Texas each had only two ministers present, representing two presbyteries in each synod. The Synod of Nashville had two ministers, representing two presbyteries, and one elder from one of those presbyteries.

The Synod of Mississippi, however, was relatively well represented, with a minister from each presbytery (two from the Presbytery of New Orleans) but no ruling elders. The Northern Synods generally had full representation (the Synod of Philadelphia, for example, had, for its seven presbyteries, fourteen ministers and fourteen ruling elders).[17] Clearly, the civil and political situation of the day marked the character of the assembly: the 1861 Old School General Assembly in Philadelphia was overwhelmingly Northern in its composition from the beginning. And at least in the judgment of Charles Hodge, the 1861 General Assembly addressed political matters that ought to have been left to the discretion of the individual members of the church.

Ironically, the moderator of the previous General Assembly, who customarily preaches the opening sermon of the new assembly (and

---

that Philadelphia was the chosen city was ironic: it was the cradle both of American Presbyterianism (being the location of the first presbytery in 1706 and the site of the first General Assembly in 1789) and of the nation (in which city both the Declaration of Independence, 1776, and the Constitution, 1789, were adopted). It was also quite a patriotic city and made it difficult to resist patriotic demands on the 1861 General Assembly to issue a strongly pro-Union statement.

15 *Minutes of the General Assembly of the Presbyterian Church in the United States of America, A.D. 1861* (Philadelphia: Presbyterian Board of Publications, 1861), 296–97.

16 *Minutes of the General Assembly, 1861*, 296–97. Eighteen counties in northwestern Virginia refused to secede and formed the state of West Virginia, which was admitted to the Union in 1863 (to the delight of President Lincoln).

17 *Minutes of the General Assembly, 1861*, 294.

presides until a new moderator is elected), preached on John 18:36, "My kingdom is not of this world," one of the classic texts ordinarily used by those vying for the doctrine of the spirituality of the church.[18] One suspects that this might have been an attempt—arguably a fruitless one—to lower the temperature of patriotic fervor and focus everyone on the ecclesiastical tasks at hand. On Saturday morning, May 18, "Dr. [Gardiner] Spring offered a resolution, that a Special Committee be appointed to inquire into the expediency of this Assembly making some expression of their devotion to the Union of these States, and their loyalty to the [Federal] Government [of the United States]; and if in their judgment it is expedient so to do, they report what that expression shall be."[19]

The resolutions that the General Assembly adopted in its final form are as follows:

Gratefully acknowledging the distinguished bounty and care of Almighty God towards this favored land, and also recognizing our obligations to submit to every ordinance of man for the Lord's sake, this General Assembly adopts the following resolutions:

1. *Resolved*, That in view of the present agitated and unhappy condition of this country, the first day of July next be hereby set apart as a day of prayer throughout our bounds; and that on that day ministers and people are called on humbly to confess and bewail our national sins; to offer our thanks to the Father of light for his abundant and undeserved goodness to us as a nation; to seek his guidance and blessing upon our rulers and their counsels, as well as on the Congress of the United States about to assemble; and to implore Him, in the name of Jesus

18 *Minutes of the General Assembly, 1861*, 294.
19 *Minutes of the General Assembly, 1861*, 303.

Christ, the great High Priest of the Christian profession, to turn away his anger from us, and speedily restore to us the blessings of an honorable peace.

2. *Resolved*, That this General Assembly, in the spirit of that Christian patriotism which the Scriptures enjoin, and which has always characterized this Church, do hereby acknowledge and declare our obligations to promote and perpetuate, so far as in us lies, the integrity of these United States, and to strengthen, uphold, and encourage the Federal Government in the exercise of all its functions under our noble Constitution; and to this Constitution in all its provisions, requirements, and principles, we profess our unabated loyalty.

And to avoid all misconception, the Assembly declare that by the terms "Federal Government," as here used, is not meant any particular administration, *or* the peculiar opinions of any particular party, but that central administration, which being at any time appointed and inaugurated according to the forms prescribed in the Constitution of the United States, is the visible representative of our national existence.

On a motion to adopt this report the *ayes* and *nays* were ordered.

The *ayes* are as follows: *Ministers*, 87; *Elders*, 69. *Total ayes*, 156.

The *nays* are as follows: *Ministers*, 49; *Elders*, 17. *Total nays*, 66.[20]

Hodge did not contest the right of the church to give prophetic witness to a matter that might have political consequences, for example, as in the case of Sabbath observance or the acknowledgment of the Christian faith in the public schools.[21] What he

---

20 *Minutes of the General Assembly, 1861*, 329–30.
21 Strange, *Spirituality of the Church*, 142–62.

contested in the action of the General Assembly in the Gardiner Spring Resolutions was the right of the church to decide for its members to whom their allegiance belonged, whether to the Union and the federal government or to their states and the government of the Confederate States of America. For his own part, Hodge made it abundantly clear in his writing and in the debate on the floor of the General Assembly over the Gardiner Spring Resolutions that he was a fervent Lincoln supporter and an ardent Union man. Nevertheless, because he firmly believed that the Gardiner Spring Resolutions decided a political question, something no assembly should do, Hodge, and those who joined him in protest, put it like this:

> We make this protest, not because we do not acknowledge loyalty to our country to be a moral and religious duty, according to the word of God, which requires us to be subject to the powers that be; nor because we deny the right of the Assembly to enjoin that, and all other like duties, on the ministers and churches under its care; but because *we deny the right of the General Assembly to decide the political question, to what government the allegiance of Presbyterians as citizens is due, and its rights to make that decision a condition of membership in our Church.*[22]

Given that the General Assembly, on the one hand, was lacking most of her Southern commissioners, it seemed arguably unfair for the Northern commissioners, in their absence, to ram through measures that Southerners would have opposed and that would have required them to give allegiance to the federal government

22 *Minutes of the General Assembly, 1861*, 339 (emphasis mine).

as opposed to their state governments. And for those Southern commissioners who were there, the passage of these resolutions defined their loyalty for them, calling them to give their loyalty to the federal government over their own states. The assembly was asking her Southern commissioners, and even more so all her Southern members, to declare their allegiance to a government hostile to their own more local government. One might think of it this way: to the degree that any Southerners would have taken up and acted on the Gardiner Spring Resolutions, to that degree the Southerners' state and the Confederate States of America as an entity could rightfully have looked on them as traitors or as treasonous. Hodge acknowledged in the protest the reality of the matter:

It is, however, a notorious fact, that many of our ministers and members conscientiously believe that the allegiance of the citizens of this country is primarily due to the States to which they respectively belong; and, therefore, that when any State renounces its connection with the United States, and its allegiance to the Constitution, the citizens of that State are bound by the laws of God to continue loyal to their State, and obedient to its laws. The paper adopted by the Assembly virtually declares, on the other hand, that the allegiance of the citizens is due to the United States; anything in the Constitution, or ordinances, or laws of the several States to the contrary notwithstanding.[23]

Hodge argued that "in adopting this paper, therefore, the Assembly does decide the great political question which agitates

23 *Minutes of the General Assembly, 1861,* 339.

and divides the country." And in so doing, Hodge contended, the General Assembly "pronounces or assumes" a particular interpretation of the US Constitution. Hodge protested flatly that "this is a matter clearly beyond the jurisdiction of the Assembly." It was beyond the jurisdiction of the assembly because it was not a matter clearly addressed in either the Scriptures or the Westminster Standards. Indeed, the Bible did ordain due submission to lawful authority, but *in a case like this, the Bible did not clearly establish which was the lawful authority.* Hodge continued:

> The General Assembly in thus deciding a political question, and in making that decision practically a condition of membership to the Church, has, in our judgment, violated the Constitution of the Church, and usurped the prerogative of its Divine Master. We protest loudly against the action of the Assembly, because it is a departure from all its previous actions. The General Assembly has always acted on the principle that the Church has no right to make anything a condition of Christian or ministerial fellowship, which is not enjoined or required in the Scriptures and the Standards of the Church.[24]

The church has no authority from her Master or competency as an institution to make such pronouncements. And this resolution made it impossible for her Southern members to continue in and with her. Instead, Southerners were "forced to choose between allegiance to their States and allegiance to their Church." Hodge believed strongly that this was neither constitutional nor neces-

---

24 *Minutes of the General Assembly, 1861,* 340.

sary and lamented that this sealed the division of the church and furthered the division of the nation.[25]

Though Thornwell had differed with Hodge in the previous two years on what precisely constituted the spirituality of the church, here he was in full agreement with and appreciative of Hodge.[26] With the coming of the war, however, the doctrine of the spirituality of the church would receive continual challenge and, in Hodge's hands, take on greater subtlety. Even though Thornwell and his Southern supporters would become particularly identified

25 William McMichael put the cost of opposing the Gardiner Spring Resolutions quite poignantly: "You and I, and other by our actions in the General Assembly, [it was alleged] *endorsed the doctrine of secession as held by the South.* Even in our Presbytery, which met a few days ago, several intelligent persons maintained that our 'Protest' held this doctrine. I, of course, declared that we held to no such thing, and explained that we simply refused to decide a political question, and voted that every man, North and South, should settle the question of allegiance for himself; that we voted as we did, because the General Assembly had no right to decide a political question; because it was 'cruel' to commit the Southern brethren to a position in which they would be compelled to sacrifice their allegiance to the Church or their allegiance to their States; and for other reasons. I also declared that the 'Protest' saved the church from an immediate rupture. Was I not right? The members, I think, became satisfied that our Protest did not [stem] from secession." He went on to lament, however, that though treated with courtesy in the Presbytery, he had, because of the Gardiner Spring Resolutions, been marginalized. He offered that "perhaps the Protest, owing to its brevity, is a little obscure on some points, to persons who did not hear the discussion in the Assembly." "Many cannot comprehend," he continued, "the statement that the action of the Assembly makes a *new term of communion.*" He looked forward to the "next repertory," which would contain the customary General Assembly analysis by Hodge, particularly of the four following questions: "1. Do the Scriptures or the Standards of our church contain a single word which encourages Ecclesiastical bodies to engage in political discussions? 2. Do the Scriptures contain one word which encourages *war* for any purposes whatever? 3. Ought the church to become a war party in any circumstance whatever?" And "4. Did not the late General Assembly virtually make a declaration of war, and in place of filling the Scriptural office of 'Peacemaker' abandon itself to the spirit of a contentious and ungodly world?" William McMichael to Charles Hodge, 26 June 1861, box 28, folder 23, CHMC.

26 This is not to imply that Thornwell was present at this assembly. Like most Southerners, he did not attend this assembly; his native state, South Carolina, had seceded from the Union months earlier, and the war had already begun in the month before the assembly.

with advocating the doctrine of the spirituality of the church, it is the case that at the point of secession, and once it had occurred, Thornwell himself addressed issues of concern that had clear political implications and ramifications in and for the new Southern Presbyterian Church (what would become the PCUS). Thornwell, in other words, could and did address the political when he perceived a moral imperative to do so.[27]

27 On the circumstances that prompted Thornwell to modify his own doctrine of the spirituality of the church, see Strange, *Spirituality of the Church*, 250–57.

4

The Spirituality of the Church and the General Assemblies of 1862–1865

IN THE TWO PRECEDING CHAPTERS, we surveyed American slavery and the rise of the Old School doctrine of the spirituality of the church. We also saw that Charles Hodge developed his own version of this doctrine at the 1861 General Assembly. Hodge earlier opposed the doctrine, as he did with issues at the 1859 and 1860 assemblies, when it was adduced to keep the church from addressing matters in civil society that he believed appropriate for the church. He supported and promoted the spirituality of the church, however, in 1861 and in the following years, when he believed that politics were improperly intruding into the church, that is, when he believed that the partisan affairs of state were being given undue consideration in the courts of the church.[1]

---

1   Hodge's views on the Civil War and on the role of the church in the Civil War can be seen in his correspondence, particularly with his brother, Hugh L. Hodge, in box 12, folder 3, CHP, Department of Rare Books and Special Collections, Princeton University Library.

Hodge held that Christians must resist an improper intrusion of politics into the courts or pulpits of the church; personally, however, he was deeply interested and even involved in politics. He had many political connections and was first an ardent Federalist, then a Whig, then a Free-Soiler, and finally a Republican.[2] Hodge believed that politics as such, that which might divide good Christians (e.g., whether to support Andrew Jackson or another politician), had no place in the public witness of the church. This does not mean that Hodge opposed the idea of the church as an institution taking moral stands that might have civil ramifications with which all good (Christian) men and women would agree.[3]

What we see in this chapter is how both civil consequences more broadly considered and politics more narrowly conceived came to have a greater role in the life of the Northern Presbyterian Church during the Civil War, which lasted from 1861 to 1865.[4] We have already looked at 1861 in the preceding chapter; thus, we begin here in 1862 and work our way through 1865. What we see in this chapter is how carefully Hodge navigated these waters in subtly developing his version of the spirituality of the church,

2 Strange, *Spirituality of the Church*, chap. 2. See Richard J. Carwardine, "The Politics of Charles Hodge," in *Charles Hodge Revisited: A Critical Appraisal of His Life and Work*, ed. John W. Stewart and James H. Moorhead (Grand Rapids, MI: Eerdmans, 2002), 247–97. See also the estimate of his son A. A. and citations in letters from Charles to his brother, Hugh, with respect to politics in A. A. Hodge, *The Life of Charles Hodge, D.D., LL.D.* (New York: Charles Scribner's Sons, 1880), esp. 230–34.

3 As was true for Hodge, especially during this period; see Hodge, *Life of Charles Hodge*, 460–81.

4 The Civil War greatly affected Hodge, as it did the nation. There are a series of letters from Hodge, particularly to his brother, Hugh, dealing with war matters, sometimes in technical detail. Hodge's fascination with the conduct of the war, and his hope for the success of the Union can be seen in letters to Hugh dealing with a variety of generals and battles in 1861–1862, found in box 12, folder 2, CHP. This continues in box 12, folder 3, which covers the rest of the war, including a letter dated April 15, 1865, from Charles to Hugh lamenting President Lincoln's assassination.

seeking to avoid the Scylla of refusing to address civil issues when necessary (as he perceived Thornwell and Robinson doing in their version of the doctrine) and the Charybdis of the politicization of the church.[5] Hodge became a veritable Duns Scotus (*doctor subtilis*) in distinguishing what is appropriate and what is not appropriate before the courts of the church, primarily in the cases we examine that were occurring in its highest court, the General Assembly.

There has never been a time in American history like those years of the US Civil War, and the churches were not left unscarred by them.[6] It was hard to resist bringing matters political into the sanctuary, and many did not even try to hold back. But Hodge always tried, as this chapter demonstrates.[7] It is hardly a surprise that the

5 In a letter to his former student Phineas D. Gurley (pastor of New York Avenue Presbyterian Church—the church that President Lincoln attended when in the White House) asking Gurley to help him obtain a commission for his son John B. Hodge as a second lieutenant, Charles Hodge even took care to say, "I can well understand that there may be reasons why you as a clergyman might not wish to interfere in such matters." Charles Hodge to Phineas D. Gurley, 2 December 1861, box 28, folder 64, CHMC, Special Collections, Princeton Theological Seminary Library. One might well wonder if, through Gurley, from whom Lincoln sought counsel on several important occasions, Hodge's doctrine of the spirituality of the church had influence on the president, particularly since Lincoln's Second Inaugural Address and proposed Reconstruction policies seem to reflect such Old School Presbyterian and Hodge-like themes.

6 C. C. Goen ably makes the point that the failure of the churches to maintain union sealed the nation's fate as it moved to civil war. Goen, *Broken Churches, Broken Nation: Denominational Schisms and the Coming of the Civil War* (Macon, GA: Mercer University Press, 1985). Not only did the churches contribute to the war, however; the war itself poured back into the churches and politicized them to a hitherto unknown degree. See, among others, Harry S. Stout, *Upon the Altar of the Nation: A Moral History of the Civil War* (New York: Viking, 2006), chaps. 13 and 26.

7 Even as Hodge would be criticized by a Thornwell or a Robinson for allowing too much in the way of politics into the church, David Neil Murchie criticizes Hodge for being too concerned with individual conversion and personal ethics and not enough with larger societal concerns; see Murchie, "Morality and Social Ethics in the Thought of Charles Hodge" (PhD diss., Drew University, 1980), esp. 349–62. Murchie does, however, see Hodge as best transcending this limitation during the Civil War and beginning there to address the social implications of Christianity (362–67).

most momentous event in American history would not leave the churches untouched. Some believe that the events of our own times, particularly the extremism that has developed on both ends of the political spectrum, likewise threatens to permeate all areas, even matters like sports and the fine arts, historically impervious to pervasive politicization. Some pundits, more often those on the left, have gone so far as to think some sort of civil war likely. The recent decades have witnessed widespread politicization that makes one long for the river of politics to return to its own banks and stop inundating every other sphere of existence (the arts, media, sports, etc.). The church is not exempt from this political flooding—hence the need to recapture a balanced doctrine of the spirituality of the church that might help us escape the pervasive politicization that currently swamps the whole of American culture.

The General Assembly of 1862

When the Gardiner Spring Resolutions passed in 1861, a handful of Southerners attended the General Assembly. In 1862, however, the Confederate States of America had solidified, the Southern Old School Presbyterian Church had been formed, and no Southerners attended the General Assembly that met in Columbus, Ohio, in May 1862.[8] The minutes of the General Assembly of that year eerily reflect that Southern absence, listing the following synods without a single member in attendance: Virginia, North Carolina, Nashville, South Carolina, Georgia, Alabama, Mississippi, Memphis, Arkansas, and Texas.[9] No distinctly Southern sentiment would now be heard that might prompt Northern restraint in an effort

8   *The Minutes of the General Assembly of the Presbyterian Church in the United States of America, A.D. 1862* (Philadelphia: Presbyterian Board of Publications, 1862), 585.
9   *Minutes of the General Assembly, 1862,* 588–89.

to maintain the bond of union. The federal Union had been fractured in 1861, and so had the union that held together the church and with it much of what had kept raw politics out of the Old School General Assemblies—namely, the consideration that words ought ever to be moderated so as to maintain the bond of union and sustain the mutual affection that all parties bear toward one another.[10] Assemblies both North and South would find it easier to castigate each other now that the Old School Presbyterian Church was divided, given the partisan nature of civic life and the onset of a war in which those who were shortly before in sweet fellowship would now be locked in mortal combat.

The real tinderboxes, both civilly and ecclesiastically, throughout the Civil War were the border states (especially Missouri, Kentucky, and Maryland; less so West Virginia and Delaware): these states were in the Union but uneasily so, often sympathetic to the South and her way of life. These states were themselves often highly divided, having ardent Unionists as well as Copperheads (those in the Union sympathetic to the Confederacy). How highly personal and political matters often were in the border states was seen right away at the 1862 General Assembly in matters brought before it from Kentucky men, particularly two (formerly) fellow professors at Danville Theological Seminary, Robert J. Breckinridge and Stuart Robinson.[11] Breckinridge presented a paper seeking to bring

10 Peter J. Wallace, " 'The Bond of Union': The Old School Presbyterian Church and the American Nation, 1837–1861" (PhD diss., University of Notre Dame, 2004). Wallace's thesis, well-developed and amply supported by a plethora of original sources (particularly from the then-contemporary religious press), demonstrates that as long as the Old School Presbyterian Church held together, so did the nation. The Old School Presbyterian Church, in other words, by remaining united long after the Baptists and Methodists had separated in the 1840s, served as a bond, a glue, that helped hold the nation together.

11 Lewis G. Vander Velde, *The Presbyterian Churches and the Federal Union, 1861–1869* (Cambridge, MA: Harvard University Press, 1932), 189–95.

a matter before the 1862 General Assembly that reflected real tensions between him and Robinson.[12]

Hodge, in his analysis of the 1862 General Assembly, navigated a marvelously narrow course as he continued to develop his doctrine of the spirituality of the church in the aftermath of his opposition to the Gardiner Spring Resolutions (at the 1861 General Assembly). On the one hand, he argued that Breckinridge's paper was lawful in a way that the Gardiner Spring Resolutions had not been: whereas the latter decided the political question in a church still composed of members North and South, Breckinridge's paper was not political *in the same way* since it addressed an already divided church, the Northern Presbyterian Church, a denomination wholly within the borders of a nation now under the US government. On the other hand, Hodge questioned the necessity and wisdom of the Breckinridge paper, arguing that it would have been better had it never been presented to the General Assembly. Hodge, in other words, argued that while Breckinridge's paper could not properly be opposed on the ground of principle, it could, and should, be on the ground of wisdom and expediency.

Hodge believed that the "wisest, most dignified, benevolent, and Christian course for the Assembly, would have been entire silence on the disturbed state of the country." Why? Because there was simply no need for this expression from Presbyterians, particularly

---

12 Robert J. Breckinridge is one of the most important Old School Presbyterians of the time, playing a formative role in the Old School–New School division of 1837 and in many of the controversies that followed in the Old School Presbyterian Church; see Edgar Caldwell Mayse, "Robert Jefferson Breckinridge: American Presbyterian Controversialist" (PhD diss., Union Theological Seminary, 1974). Stuart Robinson's life and work are set forth and defended in Preston D. Graham Jr., *A Kingdom Not of This World: Stuart Robinson's Struggle to Distinguish the Sacred from the Secular during the Civil War* (Macon, GA: Mercer University Press, 2002).

when "men so eminent for goodness, wisdom, experience, and position, as Judge Gamble, Dr. Backus . . . , Dr. McPheeters . . . , and others, from the border states, expressed their firm conviction that its adoption would injure the cause of Christ and his church in those states." For Hodge that was enough to satisfy him that "its introduction was unwise."[13] These and like observations, however, were pastoral and charitable in nature, coming from the beneficence for which Hodge was so well known, and thus did not materially speak to his sense that the Breckinridge paper, while perhaps unwise, was nonetheless acceptable from the standpoint of the spirituality of the church.

Hodge wanted to make sure that his readers kept two things in mind as he dealt with Breckinridge's paper. The first was the danger of abandoning biblical principles and embracing what he called "abolitionism." The second had to do, essentially, with the spirituality of the church, particularly as this had developed in Hodge's thinking in recent years: "Another principle which it is especially necessary that we should preserve in its integrity is the authority and prerogative of the church."[14] Hodge set forth this doctrine in tones that might please Stuart Robinson:

It is the doctrine of the Scriptures and of the Presbyterian Church, that the kingdom of Christ is not of this world; that it is not subject as to faith, worship, or discipline, to the authority of the state; and that it has no right to interfere with the state, or give ecclesiastical judgment in matters pertaining to state policy.[15]

13 Charles Hodge, "The General Assembly," *BRPR* 34, no. 3 (1862): 518–19.
14 Hodge, "General Assembly" (1862): 522.
15 Hodge, "General Assembly" (1862): 522.

Hodge then continued in a broader vein:

> It is no less, however, the doctrine of the Scriptures, that the
> church is God's witness on earth, and has the right to bear testi-
> mony against all error in doctrine and all sin in practice, whether
> in magistrate or people. The clear principle of discrimination
> between what the church may, and what it may not do, is this.
> Any question which is to be decided by the teachings of the
> word of God, the church may, and when the occasion calls for
> it, is bound to decide, and to urge or enforce that decision by
> her spiritual authority. All questions, which are to be decided by
> any other standard, lie beyond her jurisdiction.[16]

Having set forth what he believed constituted the true spirituality of the church—its proper province—Hodge attacked what he
saw as the false spirituality of the church. "In opposition to these
plain principles, there are some among us, who assert that the
church is *so purely spiritual*, it cannot pronounce judgment, or in
any way rightfully interfere, either in the pulpit or church courts,
in reference to any political question."[17] Hodge then recalled his
entry into this debate in his tangle with James Henley Thornwell,
about whom he spoke without naming him, saying contemptu-
ously, "The church, it was said, is so spiritual that she . . . cannot
condemn the slave trade." But Hodge asked, "Is there nothing in
the Bible which proves man-stealing and devastating wars for the
sake of procuring slaves to be diabolically wicked?" Further, Hodge
continued, "And is it not the very object for which the church was
founded, that she should teach God's truth, and apply it to all the

16 Hodge, "General Assembly" (1862): 522–23.
17 Hodge, "General Assembly" (1862): 523 (emphasis mine).

concerns and emergencies of life, for instruction, exhortation, and consolation?"[18]

Hodge had made it clear that the church should not forbear addressing a moral matter simply because it might have civil consequences. To make it clear, though, that he knew how to steer the ship carefully between the two extremes of the politicization of the church (an increasing problem during the war) and the "hyperspirituality" of the church (of Thornwell and Robinson), Hodge articulated his careful and nuanced doctrine of the spirituality of the church:

> She has nothing to do with politics as politics, with questions of banks and tariffs, with regard to which the rule of decision is human laws or secular interests. But with all that pertains to faith and holy living it is her prerogative and duty to hold forth the word of life. On the other hand, however, it cannot be denied that zeal for a good cause, or the fervour of patriotic feeling has led, and may again lead, the church to forget the limits set to her authority as a teacher or judge.[19]

Hodge is one who throughout these years endeavored to remind the church of her proper role and the limits of her authority, jurisdiction, and competency.

He wrote with respect to the proper province of the church,

> She cannot decide whether the Salic law is in force in Spain; whether the expulsion of the Stuarts from the throne of England was lawful; whether the American Constitution recognized the right of a state to secede from the Union; or whether Louis

18 Hodge, "General Assembly" (1862): 523.
19 Hodge, "General Assembly" (1862): 523.

Napoleon was lawfully elected emperor of the French. These are all political questions, to be decided, not by the law of God, but by historical facts and human laws.[20]

Hodge went on to mention a few more examples of things that are "all without the sphere of the church's authority." He concluded his article with this bit of counsel to his readers concerning the spirituality of the church: "As in these times of agitation, we are in so much danger of forsaking the only sure and infallible rule of faith and practice, and of giving ourselves up to the control of passion, instead of principle, it becomes us to be the more thoughtful, humble, and prayerful."[21]

The General Assembly of 1865

Ultimately, Southern interests did not prevail but were soundly defeated in the US Civil War.[22] The surrender of Lee's army in April 1865 and the downfall of the Confederate States of America set the scene for the 1865 General Assembly, meeting in May 1865 in Pittsburgh, Pennsylvania. What influenced the atmosphere of this assembly was not only the defeat of the South but, perhaps more importantly, the assassination of President Lincoln.[23] Commissioners

20 Hodge, "General Assembly" (1862): 523–24.

21 Hodge, "General Assembly" (1862): 524.

22 Why the South lost the Civil War is a complicated matter. In *Why the South Lost the Civil War* (Athens: University of Georgia Press, 1986), Richard E. Beringer, Herman Hattaway, Archer Jones, and William N. Still Jr. argue for the pervasive role of religion in propping up the Confederacy and then bringing it down when religion could no longer justify slavery; see esp. chaps. 14 and 17.

23 Lincoln had been, surprisingly to some, handily reelected in November 1864 and reached perhaps the peak of his rhetorical genius and powers of analysis in the incomparable Second Inaugural Address of March 4, 1865, just weeks before the end of the war and his assassination. The address is treated in many places and is called "Lincoln's Sermon on the Mount" by Ronald C. White in "Lincoln's Sermon on the Mount: The Second Inaugural,"

came to this General Assembly both as victors and as mourners.[24] Had Lincoln not been murdered, it may well have been the case that commissioners would have come to the General Assembly in the same way that much of the country presumably would have come to Reconstruction: generous in victory, urged on by the sympathetic Lincoln. The general view of the country in light of Lincoln's murder, however, was that "Lincoln was magnanimous in victory, clearly intent on showing kindness to the South, and this is the thanks he gets—struck down by an assassin's bullet." The kindness that many Northerners felt after Lee's surrender at Appomattox Court House evaporated when Lincoln was shot at Ford's Theatre in Washington, DC, on April 14, 1865, dying the next morning.[25]

These affairs were very much on the minds of the commissioners at the 1865 General Assembly as they gathered, prompting it to adopt a paper expressing thanks to God for the victory of the United States and for the leadership of President Lincoln, while at the same time mourning his loss. Hodge had joined in the times both of thanksgiving and of mourning, rejoicing at Lee's surrender and weeping copiously upon being informed of the president's death.[26]

---

in *Religion and the American Civil War*, ed. Randall M. Miller, Harry S. Stout, and Charles Reagan Wilson (New York: Oxford University Press, 1998), 208–25.

24 The General Assembly, on the one hand, rejoiced "concerning the triumph of our national arms" and, on the other hand, had "deep sorrow in reference to the death of Abraham Lincoln, late President of the United States." *Minutes of the General Assembly of the Presbyterian Church in the United States of America, A.D. 1865* (Philadelphia: Presbyterian Board of Publications, 1865), 531.

25 The nation had never experienced the murder of a sitting president, and coming when this did, it turned a war-weary land into a vengeful one. See Allen C. Guelzo, *Abraham Lincoln: Redeemer President* (Grand Rapids, MI: Eerdmans, 1999), 397–438. See also Edward Steers Jr., *Blood on the Moon: The Assassination of Abraham Lincoln* (Lexington: University of Kentucky Press, 2001).

26 Charles Hodge to Hugh Hodge, April 15, 1865, box 12, folder 3, CHP. See also Charles Hodge, "President Lincoln," *BRPR* 37, no. 3 (1865): 435–58; Hodge, *Life of Charles Hodge*, 482–84.

If the war had the effect of politicizing the Old School Presbyterian Church in the North, and it did, the death of Lincoln only further politicized the church. Northerners otherwise disposed to kind treatment of the returning South grew embittered and vengeful in the aftermath of the assassination. Though Hodge strongly counseled against such an attitude and urged the nation and church to imitate Lincoln's kindness, many who had lost loved ones and now the president himself were not disposed to mild treatment of the South. Moreover, this harsh spirit was not altogether absent from the General Assembly.

As Hodge noted, the matter of how to receive back the Southern church "occupied a large portion of the time of the Assembly and gave rise to protracted and excited debates."[27] The assembly was in no mood simply to receive the churches back as Lincoln wanted to receive the states back. Several measures were proposed and debated, all having in common a requirement that Southerners seeking readmittance to the Northern church ought to perform some sort of penance. Hodge feared that dictating terms in this fashion could "only serve to increase instead of allaying unfriendly and unholy feelings; to retard rather than to promote that visible union which all profess to regard an important duty."[28] Hodge was right. The requirements set down by the Northern Presbyterian Church only further politicized matters, making the reunion of the Northern and Southern churches a practical impossibility, and ultimately led the Presbyterian Church in the border states to join with the Southern Presbyterian Church in sympathy.

In answer to an overture from the Presbytery of California, the 1865 General Assembly adopted a set of requirements for South-

27 Charles Hodge, "The General Assembly," *BRPR* 37, no. 3 (1865): 496.
28 Hodge, "General Assembly" (1865): 513–14.

erners seeking readmission to the Northern church. "It is hereby ordered that all our Presbyteries examine every minister applying for admission from any Presbytery or other ecclesiastical body in the Southern States" on two points: whether the minister has freely aided or countenanced "the rebellion and the war which has been waged against the United States" and whether he "holds that the system of Negro slavery in the South is a Divine institution, and that it is 'the peculiar mission of the Southern Church to conserve the institution of slavery as there maintained.'" Thus, the assembly adopted as a rule, if a minister was guilty of one or both of these "doctrines, that he be not received without renouncing and forsaking these errors."[29] Other like conditions were laid down for ecclesiastical bodies, prospective members coming to the North from the South, and so on, all so that "most of them [the younger, less responsible Southern sympathizers], it is hoped, will be reclaimed from the error of their ways, and become loyal citizens and valuable church members."[30]

Here Hodge's subtle and nuanced doctrine of the spirituality of the church came clearly into play. Hodge understood the strong feelings of loyalty expressed at the General Assembly: "Popular bodies, whether ecclesiastical or secular, are in a great measure the organs of public spirit." And the public spirit, after four years of costly war and the assassination of the president, burned hot against the South. While "the members [of civil and ecclesiastical assemblies] may think themselves very independent, and very heroic, it may be that they are none the less swayed by outside pressure and made the organs of the spirit around them."[31] Hodge noted

29 Hodge, "General Assembly" (1865): 502.
30 Hodge, "General Assembly" (1865): 503.
31 Hodge, "General Assembly" (1865): 505.

that this was shockingly true of the supposedly more "spiritual" Southern church during the recent conflict and gave examples, lamenting, "Such is our poor human nature."[32] Further, he argued,

> It would betray great self-ignorance and self-conceit, to assume that we here at the North, and our Northern Synods and Assemblies, . . . are so elevated, so enlightened, so self-possessed, that we can rise above these disturbing elements, and think, speak, and act simply under the guidance of right principles, and of correct feeling.[33]

By such partisan and politicized sentiments, Hodge believed that the 1865 General Assembly was "carried beyond the limits of propriety in their deliverances and acts." This was not surprising to Hodge, considering "our poor human nature," but it was nonetheless disappointing.[34]

Some at the General Assembly even wanted to define loyalty as "cordial agreement with the deliverances of the Assembly on doctrine, loyalty, and freedom." In other words, some wanted to establish a rule that all deliverances of the assembly were de facto to be treated as the church's constitution—the doctrinal and polity standards—requiring agreement with all assembly statements as a proof of loyalty. Historically, however, Presbyterians in the American context had not only been permitted scruples with respect to the church's constitution but had certainly never been required to express "cordial agreement" with every motion or resolution that any given assembly might happen to adopt. This was altogether

---

32 Hodge, "General Assembly" (1865): 506.
33 Hodge, "General Assembly" (1865): 506.
34 Hodge, "General Assembly" (1865): 506.

too much for Hodge, who reminded all his readers that orthodoxy was not established by abject agreement to all that church courts did or might do, asking, "What would become of the state or the church, if minorities could not say a word in opposition to the acts of the majority?"[35]

Hodge objected that the General Assembly

> insists in authoritative acts, and requires this agreement as the condition on which the Southern ministers and presbyteries are to be received into our church. We are persuaded that not a member of the body, when he comes calmly to consider the matter, will hesitate to admit that the Assembly, in so doing, transcended its power.[36]

This is because the assembly sought by a mere declaration to amend the constitution of the church and to lay down to lower judicatories of the church the procedure that they must follow in admitting members to her, whether session, presbytery, or synod. Such an exercise of church power was unprecedented, breathtaking, and plainly over the line for Hodge, even though Hodge had always been, and ever remained, an unyielding advocate of the Union and opponent of secession. It may be noted that this sort of raw exercise of ecclesiastical power came to characterize the Presbyterian Church thereafter, with conservatives using it to require of ministerial candidates extraconstitutional affirmations in the five fundamentals of the General Assemblies of 1910, 1916, and 1923, and liberals using it to require J. Gresham Machen and those associated with him, by the 1934 General Assembly

---

35 Hodge, "General Assembly" (1865): 507.
36 Hodge, "General Assembly" (1865): 507–8.

deliverance, to repudiate involvement with the Independent Board for Presbyterian Foreign Missions.[37]

Hodge observed that General Assemblies, in keeping with the then-current *Book of Church Order*,

> allow their own members to protest against their acts, to enter their protests on the minutes; they cannot deny the right of inferior judicatories to record their dissent, nor hinder private ministers and members from condemning their action and arguing against it, and yet they [the 1865 General Assembly] declare agreement with it [in these stipulated conditions under which Southern churches, ministers and members, may return] to be a condition of ministerial and church fellowship.[38]

Hodge not only resisted undue ecclesiastical interference in civil matters as a violation of the doctrine of the spirituality of the church, but he also resisted the church exercising power that its own constitution denied to it, particularly when the church seemed to claim, as did the 1865 General Assembly in these actions, a power that was not ministerial but magisterial. Hodge, reflecting on what he viewed as high-handedness on the part of the 1865 General Assembly, provocatively said, "The popish doctrine of the infallibility of church courts does not suit Americans."[39]

Hodge argued that "the action of the Assembly with regard to the Southern churches is founded on a disregard of two plain distinctions. The one is the difference between political offenses and ordinary crimes." A wrong political theory, such as Hodge supposed

---

37 Edwin H. Rian, *The Presbyterian Conflict* (Grand Rapids, MI: Eerdmans, 1940).
38 Hodge, "General Assembly" (1865): 508.
39 Hodge, "General Assembly" (1865): 510.

the South to cherish, may lead one to be under a different government: "We are bound to obey a *de facto* government, although it be that of a usurper." Giving an example, Hodge wrote, "The present inhabitants of France are bound to recognize Louis Napoleon as emperor, whatever they may think of the revolution which placed him in power." Similarly, he noted, "The fact . . . that a man or minister supported the late wicked rebellion, is not to be assumed as a proof that he is unworthy of Christian fellowship, even if that support was voluntary on his part."[40] One must recall that this comes from a man who was an unwavering Union supporter and who had written against the South and its iniquity, as he perceived it, in the strongest and most uncompromising of terms.

The other distinction to which Hodge referred was that "between sin and ecclesiastical offences. We all have many imperfections," Hodge argued. "How often do we not see manifestations of pride, covetousness, maliciousness, arrogance, to say nothing of idleness, sloth, lukewarmness, and worldly-mindedness in ministers and church members?" Hodge thought that these reflected characteristic sins and not necessarily specific sins that were chargeable in the church courts, without rising to specific outward sins (e.g., if maliciousness manifested itself in brawling). He believed that those who were of good conscience and convinced of the Southern persuasion, while wrong, and grievously so, had not necessarily committed "ecclesiastical offenses." He wrote, "Church courts cannot visit all kinds of sins with ecclesiastical censure. We are obliged to receive all into the fellowship of the church who give evidence that they are true Christians, however imperfect they may be; otherwise, the best of us would

---

40 Hodge, "General Assembly" (1865): 511.

be excluded."[41] Only an overly agitated, partisan political spirit would fail to see this, Hodge believed.

Hodge also noted that "the demand that all who favoured the rebellion should give evidence of repentance of that sin and openly confess it, goes beyond all previous action of the Assembly, and all demands of the civil government itself." By "previous action," Hodge was referring to what the Old School required of New Schoolers wanting to return after the 1837 split (the 1869 reunion of Old and New School is dealt with in the next chapter). For now, suffice it to say that the Old School did not require the New School to repent of its errors. Hodge also noted that "the prominent advocates of the reunion of the Old and New-school Church were the most zealous in pressing through these extreme measures with regard to the Southern ministers."[42]

As for the demands of the 1865 General Assembly exceeding those of the civil government itself, that is startlingly true. Hodge wrote,

> The United States authorities require of those who participated in the rebellion, no expression of contrition, no renunciation of political theories, no avowal of approbation of the measures of the government for the preservation of the Union and abrogation of slavery, but the simple promise of obedience to the laws and allegiance to the government.[43]

This is another indication that the ecclesiastical sphere was as politicized, if not more so, than the civil one. Hodge concluded, "It seems

41 Hodge, "General Assembly" (1865): 511–12.
42 Hodge, "General Assembly" (1865): 512.
43 Hodge, "General Assembly" (1865): 513.

rather incongruous that a church court should assume to be more loyal than the government which it desires to support."[44] Again, one cannot but think that Lincoln's death embittered even Presbyterians and made them desirous of a pound of flesh. Whatever goodwill there was in those few days of March and early April 1865 after Lee's surrender but before Lincoln's death had disappeared, and the country and church were in for a rough time.[45]

We have seen Hodge develop his doctrine of the spirituality of the church. When he first encountered it in that form, in the 1859 debates at the General Assembly with Thornwell, he rejected it as a novel doctrine.[46] He enunciated, however, his own more careful version of it in 1861 in response to the Gardiner Spring Resolutions. Given the convulsions of the Civil War, the Presbyterian Church in the North tended to express itself with respect to civil matters even more during those war years than it had in 1861 or before. Hodge steered an impressive course during the war between recognizing the right of the church to address moral matters that might have political implications while resisting the church's undue plunge into matters political, particularly as seen at the 1865 General Assembly with the strict requirements placed on would-be returning Southerners. How that played out in the reunion not of North and South but of Old School and New School is the story of the next chapter.

---

44 Hodge, "General Assembly" (1865): 513.

45 A parallel can be discerned between the rougher Reconstruction that followed Lincoln's death—more stringent than any he had proposed—with the more stringent terms laid down for the reception of the Southern churches back into the Northern fold. Hodge, *Life of Charles Hodge*, 482–86.

46 See the extensive quotation from Hodge after he first encountered Thornwell's version of the spirituality of the church at the 1859 General Assembly in Strange, *Spirituality of the Church*, 257–61.

5

The Southern Church and the Reunion of the Northern Church

CHARLES HODGE, AS A CHURCHMAN who valued doctrinal soundness above all and saw it as the true basis for church unity, desired the reunion of the Northern and Southern Old School Presbyterian Churches more than anything after the war. He believed that there was a doctrinal basis for it, but the Southern church was too embittered to entertain it seriously, and the Northern church sought reunion with the New School Presbyterian Church in the North.[1] Hodge was one of the few in the North who thought that a reunion of Old and New Schools was premature.[2] He thought that if the doctrinal differences were not composed between the Old and New Schools, disaster would surely ensue, perhaps fatally

---

1   Paul C. Gutjahr contends that "the continued separation [of the Old School, North and South,] grieved Hodge as he was slow to give up his dream of seeing all Old School Presbyterians once again reunited after the war." Gutjahr, *Charles Hodge: Guardian of American Orthodoxy* (New York: Oxford University Press, 2011), 336.

2   W. Andrew Hoffecker notes that concerning the reunion of Old and New School, Hodge "found himself in the minority, and in this case a very small one." Hoffecker, *Charles Hodge: The Pride of Princeton* (Phillipsburg, NJ: P&R, 2011), 323.

compromising and corrupting what had been the Old School legacy of doctrinal fidelity.[3] The Northern Old School Church as a whole was less interested in seeking reunion with the Southern Old School Church and more with the Northern New School Church because the war had made political unity as important as, if not more important than, doctrinal and spiritual unity. It was Hodge's commitment to the spirituality of the church as he saw it that made him value doctrinal unity over political unity.[4]

The Dilemma of the Border States

As noted at the end of the last chapter, the Old School Presbyterian Church in the North had become more politicized during the war and even more so after the death of President Lincoln. Opposition to the high barrier that the Northern Presbyterian Church placed on would-be returning Southern Presbyterian churches ran especially high in the border states: the Presbytery of Louisville adopted a "Declaration and Testimony" that brought these concerns to the

3　I believe that Hoffecker is correct: "Hodge did not believe New Schoolers were heretical, but he contended that historically the New School held to a latitudinarian view of subscription." Hoffecker, *Charles Hodge*, 325. Previously, the New School had tolerated a moral government theory of the atonement and the denial of the imputation of Adam's sin and of human inability. Hodge feared that these and other doctrinal aberrations would continue as long as the New School permitted her officers to commit themselves so loosely to the Westminster Standards, while Hodge preferred a stricter commitment.

4　Gutjahr argues that "history had passed Hodge by," ironically so since Hodge had always been a voice of moderation and maintaining union, though he now opposed reunion between Old and New School in the North. Gutjahr, *Charles Hodge*, 342–43. I would argue, however, that he remained a voice of moderation (opposing harsh measures against the Old School South and border states) while hoping for reunion with the New School on the right basis. Hodge did not want to purchase the unity of the church at the expense of her peace and purity and considered reunion with the New School premature. See also the classic work on the doctrinal liberalization involved in the reunion by Princeton historian Lefferts A. Loetscher, *The Broadening Church: A Study of Theological Issues in the Presbyterian Church since 1869* (Philadelphia: University of Pennsylvania Press, 1954).

General Assembly of 1866. This document, however, did not do so in the measured tones of Hodge's version of the spirituality of the church but in the breathless ones that often characterized those who embraced what Hodge regarded as an exaggerated, overly strict view of the doctrine.

To put it another way, the extremism of the 1865 General Assembly (in placing a high bar for the readmission of the Southern churches) was met with the extremism of the spirituality of the church of Stuart Robinson and those in the border states. Hodge, in his report on the 1866 General Assembly, wrote that "the questions presented for discussion included topics in which the whole community took the liveliest interest, and the conclusions arrived at are likely to have a very great and perhaps lasting influence on the character and destiny of the Presbyterian church."[5] Hodge's assessment here appears to have proved prophetic. The Presbyterian Church chose a politicized course from which, in its mainline expression, it has never recovered.

Though Hodge believed that the church was a spiritual institution and objected to the Gardiner Spring Resolutions, he found this Louisville Presbytery document odious. Hodge assessed the "hyperspirituality" document in this fashion:

> The severity of its language, its sweeping assertions, its charges of defection and heresy against the supreme judicatory of the church, its condemnation of principles and practices coeval with our organization, and its avowed schismatical object, offended the judgment and conscience of the great body of our members, ministers, and elders.[6]

5 Charles Hodge, "The General Assembly," *BRPR* 38, no. 3 (1866): 425.
6 Hodge, "General Assembly" (1866): 425.

Hodge also criticized the call of the "Declaration and Testimony" signatories for a counterconvention of their sympathizers to meet at the same time as the 1866 General Assembly. He said in theory that such could be done "when the appointed means of governing the church or state are deemed unworthy of confidence. In the present case, as the events show, no such emergency existed."[7]

Hodge opined that the document was "founded, from first to last, upon an erroneous theory of the office and prerogatives of the church." He disclosed that he believed, tellingly, that this "theory . . . was advanced for a purpose, and was never acted upon by any branch of the church from the beginning. It assumes the church to be so spiritual in its nature and functions that it cannot recommend objects of benevolence [external to the institutional church] . . . , nor testify against *such glaring sins as the African slave-trade*."[8] This sentence reveals two things, the first fairly unremarkable and the second stunning. First, this sentence shows that Hodge's opposition to Thornwell's version of the spirituality of the church remained firm, but second, and quite shockingly, Hodge spoke of the African slave trade, rather laconically, as a sin.

Hodge spent years before the war defending slavery against charges that it was *malum in se*; here, instead of his tendentious arguments about only the abuses and not the institution as wrong, Hodge simply addressed the slave trade and called it sin. One might respond that he was addressing the slave trade narrowly and not the institution of slavery broadly. My point, however, is that he satisfied himself with just mentioning the slave trade and called it evil without laboring to defend slavery ipso facto, as he customarily did and seemed to feel compelled to do when he believed that he

7   Hodge, "General Assembly" (1866): 430.
8   Hodge, "General Assembly" (1866): 431 (emphasis mine).

must *because the Union was at stake.* Hodge did not here give the usual "This does not mean that the slavery that developed from the slave trade was evil along with the trade itself." He simply, and in welcome fashion, let his condemnation rest without qualification on African slavery.

The "Declaration and Testimony," Hodge complained, "forbids all injunctions to Christians to be faithful, as citizens to the Government under which they live. It is, among other things, against the acts of the Assembly, passed during the late war, declaring the duty of loyalty and obedience to the civil authorities, that the signers of this document testify."[9] Stunning as Hodge's claim sounds—since clearly the Bible enjoins Christians, ordinarily, to submit to the powers that be (Rom. 13:4)—Hodge is not wrong. If all the expressions passed by the General Assembly calling to support the nation of which they were citizens in the war they were prosecuting were, in form, illicit, then the church was forbidden from calling her members to submit to the state. Hodge asserted, "If this doctrine were to prevail, a seal would be set on the lips of the church, and she would be forbidden to testify against many sins and to enjoin many duties which lie properly within her sphere."[10]

Hodge rejected this approach of the Louisville Presbytery and those in agreement with it: "In consequence of this contracted view of the prerogative of the church, the Declaration refuses all regard not only to such acts and deliverances of the Assembly as may really transcend the limits of the constitution, but to many which are perfectly legitimate."[11] Clearly, Hodge did not believe that the church enjoyed carte blanche and could do as it pleased.

9   Hodge, "General Assembly" (1866): 431.
10 Hodge, "General Assembly" (1866): 431.
11 Hodge, "General Assembly" (1866): 431.

She was to operate within constitutional bounds. The signatories to the "Declaration and Testimony," however, saw those constitutional bounds as so restrictive that the church was bound and gagged from proclaiming the whole counsel of God. Hodge clearly rejected what he regarded a radical version of the doctrine of the spirituality of the church.[12]

Hodge, the moderate, wanted those who held to what he took to be an extreme doctrine of the spirituality of the church to be checked by the assembly. At the same time, he wanted the assembly to check itself and to maintain the proper bounds and limits of the church and not to politicize or further polarize matters needlessly.[13] Hodge's greatest desire was for reunion of the whole Old School, North and South, so it was in his interest in the aftermath of the war, as Lincoln had believed it to be in his interest in the little time that he had after Lee's surrender, to downplay differences between North and South, not seeking to exacerbate but to ameliorate them with a view to reuniting.[14] This is why Hodge, though ultimately siding with the assembly in its condemnation of the sentiments expressed in the "Declaration and Testimony," also had some measure of sympathy for all the parties involved in the dispute.

Professor Hodge was not slow to respond to those who would have likened him in his opposition to Gardiner Spring to the signatories of the "Declaration and Testimony"; as Hodge put it, "It tends however to nothing but confusion and misrepresentation to

12 Hodge, "General Assembly" (1866): 431.
13 Hodge believed that the assembly should have restrained itself more in some of its actions and expressions with respect to the "Declaration and Testimony" and the Louisville Presbytery, though in the main Hodge agreed with the final actions of the 1866 General Assembly.
14 Gutjahr, *Charles Hodge*, 336–42; Hoffecker, *Charles Hodge*, 317–28; A. A. Hodge, *The Life of Charles Hodge, D.D., LL.D.* (New York: Charles Scribner's Sons, 1880), 501–8.

confound things essentially different."[15] Rather, Hodge maintained, "There is as much difference between the protest to the Assembly of 1861" and "the Declaration and Testimony [of 1866]" as there is "between Dr. R. J. Breckinridge and Dr. Stuart Robinson."[16] Breckinridge had joined Hodge in protesting Gardiner Spring, together staking out what one might call a moderate doctrine of the spirituality of the church, while Stuart Robinson was the leader of the extreme "spirituality of the church" party.

Hodge reprised the purpose of protesting the Gardiner Spring Resolutions: "The subject matter of the action, in the premises, being purely political, was incompetent to a spiritual court."[17] It is clear that, for Hodge, only church action that is "purely political"—not merely an action that has some political consequences—violates the spirituality of the church. Churches may take actions that have some political ramifications as long as they are biblical actions: a minister may preach against laws forbidding slaves to read, and a church judicatory may pass a resolution calling for allowing slaves to be taught to read. Political consequences may attach to such actions, but Hodge was not concerned about that. What he wanted the church to avoid was taking actions that were purely political.[18]

After defending his and Breckinridge's opposition to the actions of the 1861 General Assembly, Hodge proceeded to contrast their actions with those of the 1866 signatories of the "Declaration and Testimony." He argued that those, like himself, who opposed Gardiner Spring in 1861 could stay "in perfect consistency with their

---

15 Hodge, "General Assembly" (1866): 431.
16 Hodge, "General Assembly" (1866): 436–37.
17 Hodge, "General Assembly" (1866): 437.
18 Hodge, "General Assembly" (1866): 437.

former action"[19] when they united in the 1862–1865 General Assemblies in calling all the states that remained loyally in the Union to support their national government. Two factors had changed the situation after 1861: (1) it was no longer a concern to stave off ecclesiastical disunion, and (2) the South had formed its own Presbyterian Church.[20] Hodge held that "in this matter, therefore, there is a great gulf between the two parties," the moderates of 1861 (who opposed Gardiner Spring and went on to support a tempered version of the spirituality of the church) and the extremists of 1866.[21]

Hodge acknowledged that there were those in the Presbyterian Church who, like himself, did not approve of the actions of the 1865 General Assembly that incensed the Louisville Presbytery. Such judicatories and individuals protested against "a mere deliverance of the Assembly (not sitting in its judicial capacity) [serving as] binding on the conscience of the people." Hodge both in 1861 and 1865 had argued that "no deliverance of the Assembly therefore can be imposed as binding on the people or upon inferior judicatories, which either transcends the limits of church power, or is contrary to the constitution, or in contravention of the Word of God."[22] Here is Hodge's doctrine of the nature and limits of church power. The power of the institutional church is a power qualified by service and submission to the word of God. The church is neither to dominate nor legislate but rather to minister and declare what the Scriptures say explicitly or what may be deduced therefrom "by good and necessary consequence" (Westminster Confession of Faith 1.6).

19 Hodge, "General Assembly" (1866): 437.
20 See Hodge, "General Assembly" (1866): 438.
21 Hodge, "General Assembly" (1866): 438.
22 Hodge, "General Assembly" (1866): 438.

Hodge continued,

> Had the Declaration and Testimony confined itself to testify-
> ing in behalf of the principle in question, and confined the
> application of it to proper limits, there would have been no
> ground of complaint. But it refuses to recognize the authority
> of acts which are fully in accordance with the constitution
> and the Scriptures, and denounces as heretical doctrines
> which the Presbyterian Church has ever recognized as true
> and sound.[23]

The signatories of the "Declaration and Testimony," acting on the
basis of their doctrine of the spirituality of the church, rejected
not only the acts of the church that arguably exceeded church
power but also those that neither Hodge nor Breckinridge believed
exceeded church power.

Specifically, Hodge continued, the "Declaration and Testimony"
"testifies against all deliverances during the late war, exhorting the
people to loyalty and the support of the government. It denies that
the church, as such, owes allegiance to any human government."
Hodge noted that, in fact, the "Declaration and Testimony" went
so far as to accuse the General Assembly of "asserting the bold
Erastian heresy, that the revealed will of the Lord Jesus Christ is
the supreme law of the land."[24] Traditionally, Erastianism is that
doctrine emerging from certain states of the Reformation that the
state is over the church and that the established church is auxiliary
to the state.[25]

---

23 Hodge, "General Assembly" (1866): 439.
24 Hodge, "General Assembly" (1866): 439.
25 For a fuller treatment of Erastianism, see Strange, *Spirituality of the Church*, 16–31.

Hodge noted here that what the Louisville Presbytery denominates as Erastian is "nothing more than the assertion of a truth which all Christians admit, viz., that the will of Christ binds all men to whom it is revealed in all their circumstances and relations."[26] Even James Henley Thornwell, archdefender of the doctrine of the spirituality of the church, believed both that the word of God should prevail in the counsels of state and that civil society should confess and maintain the crown rights of King Jesus.[27] According to the "Declaration and Testimony," Hodge and Thornwell were both Erastians. This doctrine of the spirituality of the church, then, was more radical than Thornwell's and was the one, as Jack Maddex rightly notes, that came to dominate in the border states and the South in the Reconstruction era.[28]

Reiterating why the "Declaration and Testimony" was not like opposition to the acts of the Assemblies of 1861 or 1865, Hodge argued, "It is one thing, therefore, to protest against acts which transcend the constitution [as Hodge had done in 1861 and 1865], and another to pronounce nugatory or heretical acts and declarations [such as the assembly crafted and Hodge supported from 1862 to 1864] which are perfectly scriptural and constitutional."[29] Hodge continued advancing other arguments against the "Declaration and Testimony." He noted that the commissioners from the excluded Presbytery of Louisville, through the agency of friends, had a paper presented defending their actions and denying that they had openly defied the assembly. They repeated the claims that they were doing nothing but the

---

26 Hodge, "General Assembly" (1866): 439.

27 For a treatment of Thornwell's position, see Strange, *Spirituality of the Church*, 250–57.

28 Jack P. Maddex, "From Theocracy to Spirituality: The Southern Presbyterian Reversal on Church and State," *JPH* 54, no. 4 (1976): 438–39.

29 Hodge, "General Assembly" (1866): 439.

same thing that a multitude of commissioners and judicatories had done all along who opposed the "political pronouncements" of the last five assemblies.[30]

The main thing to be gathered from the Louisville Presbytery men is that they believed that the church had regularly exceeded its authority during the previous five years by making a plethora of political pronouncements that had violated the doctrine of the spirituality of the church. In fact, the heart of the "Declaration and Testimony" was that in doing so, the General Assembly had grossly trampled on the doctrine of the spirituality of the church and thus delegitimized itself. Ultimately, in response to the actions of the General Assembly,[31] not only the Louisville Presbytery but other border state judicatories withdrew from the Northern Old School Presbyterian Church and realigned with the Southern Presbyterian Church.[32] It is from that point forward that the narrower doctrine of the spirituality of the church espoused by many in the border states and exemplified by the "Declaration and Testimony" came to shape the Southern church, the Presbyterian Church in the United

30 Hodge, "General Assembly" (1866): 439–40.

31 The actions of the 1866 General Assembly were modified over the course of that assembly, beginning with a fiat dissolution of the Louisville Presbytery and four other more draconian actions, including the creation of a due process mechanism to deal with presbyters in rebellion. Most important for our purposes, the 1866 General Assembly adopted a lengthy pastoral letter to the churches defending its actions of the last five years regarding the provinces of church and state and the relationship of the assemblies during that time to the civil government, particularly the US government. This was a decisive rejection of the border state protesters' more narrowly defined spirituality of the church. *The Minutes of the General Assembly of the Presbyterian Church in the United States of America, A.D. 1866* (Philadelphia: Presbyterian Board of Publications, 1866), 39, 59–62, 82–90.

32 "The politics of Presbyterian unity," as it is termed by D. G. Hart and John R. Muether, is what drove the Southern Old and New Schools together during the war and the Northern Old and New Schools together after the war and kept the Northern and Southern Presbyterian Churches apart for more than a century. Hart and Muether, *Seeking a Better Country: 300 Years of American Presbyterianism* (Phillipsburg, NJ: P&R, 2007), 157–64.

States (PCUS).[33] This formative influence continued well into the twentieth century.[34]

This broad and all-encompassing doctrine of the spirituality of the church, reflected in the "Declaration and Testimony" and shaping the Southern church for decades to come, was not the doctrine that Hodge and other moderates embraced. Hodge's doctrine of the spirituality of the church, as we have seen, was far more modest, serving simply to define the province of the church as ecclesiastical rather than political or civil while not keeping the church from engaging in her prophetic task to declare the whole counsel of God to all, inside or outside the church.[35] The spirituality of the church, for Hodge, was a doctrine calculated to assist the church in maintaining its focus: the gathering and perfecting of the saints. It was not a doctrine whereby the church, as it were, precensored what it would address. The church was to address everything that it had biblical warrant and mandate to address and to leave the details of matters like politics and economics to its members as Christians acting individually or in concert, as long as all was governed by biblical principles.

33 This is the claim of Jack Maddex in his renowned *JPH* article "From Theocracy to Spirituality": it was after the war that the border state doctrine of the spirituality of the church, as manifested in the "Declaration and Testimony," took hold of the Southern church. While, as we've seen here, the spirituality doctrine took shape before this, it became a distinctive of the Southern Presbyterian Church, the PCUS, particularly in the postbellum years.

34 Morton H. Smith renders a jeremiad on how the Southern church was staunchly devoted to the spirituality doctrine and how the church departed from that teaching during the course of the twentieth century, embracing various aspects of what might be termed a "social gospel." Smith, *How Is the Gold Become Dim: The Decline of the Presbyterian Church, U.S., as Reflected in Its Assembly Actions* (Jackson, MS: Premier, 1973), 12–22.

35 Hodge, "General Assembly" (1866): 441–97. In the remainder of his analysis of the fate of the Louisville Presbytery and its "Declaration and Testimony" at the 1866 General Assembly, Hodge was at great pains to set forth his view of the proper doctrine of the spirituality of the church, truncated here because it is thoroughly developed above.

Church Union and the Spirituality of the Church

The last major consideration with respect to Hodge and his doctrine of the spirituality of the church is the position that he took on the reunion of the Old and New School Presbyterian Churches in the North. Several factors conspired together to bring about such a reunion in the aftermath of the Civil War.[36] One might think that Hodge, a long-time moderate and peacemaker, would have been an advocate, perhaps even a zealous advocate, of reunion. After all, he had failed to press for disunion in 1836–1837, to the dismay of hard-line conservatives like his old pastor Ashbel Green and his former student Robert J. Breckinridge, and had only reluctantly accepted the division between the Old and New School.[37] During the next thirty years, however, Hodge came to view the separation between Old and New School as serving to maintain doctrinal purity in the Old School Church—as well as helping to keep the nation united before the Civil War. Hodge believed that the New School tolerated aberrant views, even if most of its members were orthodox, and that reunion would not have the effect of purifying the New School but possibly of corrupting the Old School. He hoped that Old School–New School reunion might occur, but he thought that it should occur only when the New School insisted on greater doctrinal fidelity among its own members.

36 Gutjahr points out that what had divided Old and New School before the war seemed to recede into insignificance during and after the war. Doctrinal differences came to be seen as, at best, far less important than the political sensibilities of the new nation that emerged from the Civil War. Men in the North had fought and died together to maintain the Union, free the slaves, and be a part of the "new birth of freedom" (as Lincoln said in the Gettysburg Address). They had all this in common and none of this in common with their brethren in the Southern Old School. For this reason, many Northerners preferred Old School–New School reunion in the North rather than reunion in the Old School North and South. Gutjahr, *Charles Hodge*, 336–43.

37 See Strange, *Spirituality of the Church*, 69–73.

Hodge looked instead to a reunion between the Old School in the North and the South.[38] To him, this held out a greater promise than Northern reunion of Old School and New School and certainly would allow for greater doctrinal purity. As we have seen, however, it became evident at the war's conclusion in 1865 that any North-South reunion would not come easily.[39] The initial conciliatory attitude of Lincoln toward the South promising a mild reconstruction of the nation boosted prospects for a North-South church reunion, but Lincoln's assassination dashed all such hopes. The actions of the assemblies of 1865 and 1866, described previously, revealed an angry North whose harsh actions served only further to embitter a defeated and humiliated South. Terms of loyalty were laid down that were seen as so draconian that the border states left the Northern church and joined the Southern church. North-South church reunion for the Old School Presbyterian Church grew increasingly unlikely.[40]

38 For Hodge, the Old School–New School separation was not unreasonable given the causes for division. Still, the Northern-Southern division—caused in the church, Hodge believed, by the Gardiner Spring Resolutions—was more reparable and reasonable. Of course, the Old and New Schools in the South had reunited in 1864 (having split only in 1857) and continued after the war as a united church, the Presbyterian Church in the United States (PCUS). Hodge was willing for reunion with this united body not only because the Southern New School had been quite orthodox but because the PCUS had the same kind of confessional subscription terms as did the Northern Old School. Reunion with the PCUS would have maintained the kind of confessional Calvinism that Hodge believed necessary for doctrinal fidelity. See also Lefferts A. Loetscher, *A Brief History of the Presbyterians*, 4th ed. (Philadelphia: Westminster, 1983), 104–26.

39 Gutjahr, *Charles Hodge*, 336.

40 Though the Northern church did pull back from its harshest positions, the Southern church remained resistant. For Dabney's and other Southerners' staunch opposition to reunion with the Northern church as well as the vain entreaties from the North to reunite, something that would not occur until well over a hundred years later, see Sean Michael Lucas, *Robert Lewis Dabney: A Southern Presbyterian Life* (Phillipsburg, NJ: P&R, 2005), 150–60. Southern and Northern Presbyterians reunited in 1983, for which see the added chapter by George Laird Hunt in Loetscher, *Brief History*, 185–203.

Northern Presbyterians were, to be sure, inflamed against their Southern brethren during and after the war. The recrimination was mutual. As Paul Gutjahr notes, "Many Old School Southern Presbyterians felt both the animosity of their Northern peers and the loss of the war so keenly that they no longer desired fellowship with their Northern brethren."[41] From the perspective of Southerners, Northerners had stripped them of their dignity, fortunes, and way of life. Many Southerners were embittered, Robert Lewis Dabney serving as a prime example. A particularly telling instance occurred at the 1870 General Assembly of the Southern Presbyterian Church (the PCUS). The now reunited Northern Presbyterian Church—the Presbyterian Church in the United States of America (PCUSA)—had sent a delegation to sue for peace and to seek reconciliation. Sean Michael Lucas notes, "Fearing that the Assembly would . . . advocate fraternal relations with the Northern church, which Dabney believed to be the first step toward reunion, he raised his voice on the floor" in opposition to the overture seeking fraternal relations, and the Northern olive branch was rejected.[42] The Southern church demanded that the Northern church repudiate and renounce all the expressions deemed to violate the spirituality of the church, all the sorts of things listed in and protested against in the "Declaration and Testimony" of the Louisville Presbytery in 1866. Hodge, whose hopes for a reunion between the Northern and Southern churches were dashed by now, wrote dismissively, "The idea of undertaking to erase from the records of past Assemblies all that is offensive to us or others with whom we may have friendly relations is impracticable and absurd."[43]

---

41 Gutjahr, *Charles Hodge*, 336.

42 Lucas, *Robert Lewis Dabney*, 152.

43 Charles Hodge, "The Delegation to the Southern General Assembly," *BRPR* 42, no. 3 (1870): 449.

Obviously, the Northern Old School Presbyterian Church and the united, largely Southern Old School Presbyterian Church were more dedicated to bitterness and recrimination than to reunion, rendering Hodge's dream of Old School reunion hopeless.

Even before Hodge knew that reunion with the South was unlikely, however, he had reservations about Northern Old School–New School reunion, thinking it at best premature and at worst potentially catastrophic, especially if the question of the different degree of theological latitude between the two schools remained unaddressed.[44] The issue of reunion between the Old and New Schools in the North surfaced rather quickly after the beginning of the war. Hodge took note of this in his account of the General Assemblies of 1862 and 1863. When the subject arose at the 1862 General Assembly, the assembly seemed unready to consider the matter fully, and it was agreed to appoint a delegation to the 1863 New School General Assembly. A number of fraternal delegates from the Old School attended the New School Assembly in 1863 and made enthusiastic overtures to the New School.[45] The war was on in earnest, the North was often faring poorly, and it is not difficult to understand how beleaguered, grieving fellow Unionists—many of whom had lost sons, brothers, cousins, and so on—would feel

---

44 That is, the Old School required stricter subscription (allowing fewer exceptions) to the Westminster Standards, while the New School allowed a rather loose subscription, in which one would be permitted to deny or take issue with what Hodge and the Old School regarded as key to the system of doctrine.

45 Gutjahr notes that former Senate chaplain and Old School stalwart Septimus Tustin addressed the 1863 New School in rhapsodic language: "The strife [between the two schools] is at an end. The fierce war-cry that grated so long upon the heart of piety has died away into an echo so indistinct as scarcely distinguishable. Our ecclesiastical war-steeds, if we may so speak, are reclining amidst the olive groves of peace." War with the South made for peace with brethren in the North, and "in this spirit, the following years saw the exchange of numerous delegates between the Old and New School General Assemblies." Gutjahr, *Charles Hodge*, 338.

and would want to feel that differences between Old and New School seemed petty and insignificant in the face of such devastating carnage and loss. Hodge was able to keep his theological head even during the worst crises of the war, but for many others, former differences with the New School paled into insignificance in the face of the life-and-death challenges of the war. This became particularly the case when Lincoln made the destruction of slavery a war aim. One can imagine enough sentiment for ecclesiastical reunion when a war for union was being fought. There was even more pressure for reunion in the North when slavery—an issue that often divided Old and New School—divided the two schools less than it ever did and, finally, divided them no more.[46]

In noting that Hodge kept his head even when those about him were losing theirs, what I mean is that Hodge continued to have concerns about the doctrinal fidelity of the New School that all the exigencies of war could not erase. The horrors of war might have caused many if not most in the Old School to set aside their differences with the New School, but for Hodge, nothing was sufficient to cause him to sacrifice the theological principles that he believed separated the two schools. Hodge's reservations are reflected in several key articles, particularly an article on church union, a review of an article by Henry Boynton Smith, and a protest emerging from the reunion talks.[47]

---

46 Hodge remained an opponent of abolition (that slavery in all circumstances was wrong), as did many in the Old School, even though they rejoiced to see its end. The New School was by no means abolitionist as such, but abolitionists typically found a more comfortable home there. The war simply shortened the distance between the two, and with emancipation in 1863 and then the full abolition of slavery in 1865 (with the passage of the Thirteenth Amendment to the US Constitution), the institution of slavery was eradicated and could no longer divide the Old and New Schools.

47 Charles Hodge, "Principles of Church Union, and the Reunion of the Old and New-School Presbyterians," *BRPR* 37, no. 2 (1865): 271–313; Hodge, "*Presbyterian Reunion*, by the Rev.

Hodge did not allege that the New School was rife with theological error or that its ministers were largely unsound. His complaint was simple: the New School, at the time of the split in 1837 up to the then-present time (mid- to late 1860s), permitted certain ministers to function protected and safe in the New School even though they denied the imputation of Adam's sin, subscribed to a governmental theory of the atonement, and otherwise held quite loosely to Calvinism as a system. Hodge's argument was that even if there were few such men, the latitude given to what he regarded as aberrant views in the New School Church meant that the New School would at least tend to doctrinal looseness, if it would not permit more serious cases of error. These and other concerns are represented in the first two articles cited above. It is that last article, "The Protest and Answer," that most concisely distills Hodge's alarm.[48]

The protest itself, issued by those who shared Hodge's position, noted,

> The first article of the plan proposes that "the reunion shall be effected on the doctrinal and ecclesiastical basis of our common standards," . . . it being understood that various methods of viewing, stating, explaining, and illustrating the doctrines of the Confession, which do not impair the integrity of the Reformed or

---

Henry B. Smith, D.D. Reprinted from the *American Presbyterian and Theological Review*, October 1867," *BRPR* 40, no. 1 (1868): 53–83; Hodge, "The Protest and Answer," *BRPR* 40, no. 3 (1868): 456–77.

48 The "Protest and Answer" article followed the 1868 General Assembly and recorded in full both a protest against the terms of the proposed reunion (with which Hodge—who did not attend the 1868 General Assembly—had full sympathy) and the General Assembly's answer to the protest, as well as Hodge's analysis of the protest. Hodge here again made clear that he was not opposed to reunion if based on the simple terms that both schools adopt the Westminster Standards without qualification.

Calvinistic system, are to be freely allowed in the united church as they have been hitherto allowed in the separate churches.[49]

The protesters observed, "Under this term of the compact, we shall be bound to allow all those forms of doctrine which the New-school Church has hitherto allowed."[50] Those protesting made it clear that they opposed these terms of reunion with the New School "because it utterly unsettles our standard of doctrine," making it dependent on what had been allowed in either church at any time, thus necessarily setting the parameters for doctrinal divergence as broad as the New School ever made it.[51]

To be clear, what was being proposed as—and became—the basis of reunion between the Old School and the New School in the North was that whatever had been acceptable in either the Old School or the New School Churches before the proposed reunion would be acceptable after it. This kind of "least common denominator approach" was unacceptable to Hodge and those protesting.[52] Hodge was unwilling for a reunited church in the North to have to accommodate New School aberrations when the Old School had never been willing to do so. This proposed union was clearly on New School terms since anything ever permitted in the New School would now have to be permitted in the new reunited church.

---

49 Hodge, "Protest and Answer," 456.

50 Hodge, "Protest and Answer," 456.

51 Hodge, "Protest and Answer," 456.

52 The article, with such terms of reunion, according to the protest, "binds us to approve of doctrines which our General Assembly has formally condemned." Hodge, "Protest and Answer," 456. The complaint here is that by joining with the New School on New School terms, the Old School effectively disappears, and anything permitted by the New School must be permitted in the reunited church.

Those protesting, like Hodge, made it clear, "We distinctly disavow any intention of imputing error in doctrine to the mass of our New-school brethren . . . [and] disavow any impeachment of their sincerity or integrity," yet they nonetheless noted that while the New School as an aggregate did not teach such error, it had permitted error to proceed unchecked.[53] The protest proceeded to list "some of the more important of the errors" thus allowed to be held by New School men, running to eight major errors or categories of errors.[54] Again, the protest affirmed, "We are far from believing . . . that these doctrines are generally approved by the New-school Church."[55] But some New School men, here or there, from time to time, had been permitted to hold one or more of these errors, while at the same time adopting the Westminster Standards, to which these errors stood opposed, as their own confession of faith. Hodge and the others feared, rightly, that this meant that in a reunited church, what had been allowed in the New School would be argued as acceptable in the reunited church.

Those bringing the protest made other points, especially concerning polity and constitution, that are not particularly germane to our argument.[56] Likewise, Hodge's reporting of the assembly's "Answer to the Protest"[57] and his analysis of both the protest and

---

53 Hodge, "Protest and Answer," 456–57.

54 The eight errors have to do with the denial of the following: Adam's original righteousness, the covenant of works and Adam's headship, original sin and its transmission, man's inability as fallen, the monergistic nature of regeneration, unconditional election, the penal-substitutionary atonement of Christ, and justification as involving the imputation of Christ's righteousness. Hodge, "Protest and Answer," 457–58.

55 Hodge, "Protest and Answer," 459.

56 Hodge, "Protest and Answer," 459–61.

57 Hodge, "Protest and Answer," 461–67. The General Assembly indignantly argued that it was absurd to think that the New School could permit the kinds of errors that the protest

answer are also not particularly relevant to our point.[58] The argument here is that Hodge wanted, vainly, union with a doctrinally faithful Southern Old School Church more than he did with a theologically compromised Northern New School Church because of his spiritual conception of the church. Recall from previous chapters that Hodge's view of the church was that it was in its essence spiritual and thus at its heart doctrinal.[59] Hodge always privileged doctrine or content over polity or form. For Hodge, a church should join with another church because it substantively agrees in doctrine, not because, as Hodge put it, "the essential bond is the form of government."[60] Here Hodge contrasted directly such a bond with one whose bond of union is "the form of doctrine." Hodge saw the Roman Catholic Church and the Anglican Church, for instance, as ones whose bond of union is governmental, involving, among other things, submission to the bishop of Rome, in the case of the former, and submission to the English sovereign, in the case of the latter. He contrasted these churches with those churches, including (he held) Presbyterian churches, "where the greatest stress is laid upon doctrine."[61]

---

alleged that it did and remain at all confessional or Calvinistic, going so far as to characterize the alleged errors as "Pelagian" or "Arminian." The General Assembly largely passed over the contention that the reunion as proposed would be brought to pass on New School terms.

58 Hodge, "Protest and Answer," 468–77. Hodge expressed utter incredulity that the General Assembly refused to take notice of, or acknowledge, those in the New School who had imbibed the errors that the protest cited. In other respects, Hodge made it clear that he opposed the apparent willingness of the majority in the Old School to reunite at any price rather than both sides coming together on the basis of the Westminster Standards held honestly and in integrity.

59 For Hodge's perspective on the spiritual, doctrinal nature of the church, over against an outward and overly objectified view of the church, see Strange, *Spirituality of the Church*, chaps. 3, 4, and 6.

60 Hodge, "*Presbyterian Reunion*, by the Rev. Henry B. Smith," 53.

61 Hodge, "*Presbyterian Reunion*, by the Rev. Henry B. Smith," 53.

CHAPTER 5

Hodge proceeded in this article to argue that since the Presbyterian churches laid greatest stress on doctrinal unity, any contemplated union should attend to doctrine; the proposed union, however, with the New School church on New School terms, which were doctrinally lax, did not attend to such a distinction. Hodge was not interested in uniting with a church that might have the same organization but permitted doctrinal latitude that compromised its purity.[62] He feared that if the Old and New Schools came together as quickly as was proposed, trouble would inevitably follow.[63] All this is to say that Hodge's opposition to the reunion of the Old and New School Churches on New School terms can be seen as of a piece with his doctrine of the spirituality of the church, in which he was concerned more with true spiritual unity, which to him meant doctrinal unity, than mere outward unity. And the political pressure for such unity—"We fought a war together against the South; can we not now unify, having been political and military cobelligerents? Can we not be ecclesiastical allies?"—had little purchase with Hodge, ardent Unionist though he was, because of his doctrine of the spirituality of the

62 Hodge, "*Presbyterian Reunion*, by the Rev. Henry B. Smith," 54–55.
63 The Old School–New School reunion, set in motion by the actions of the 1868 General Assembly, was accomplished in 1869 by a unanimous vote in the New School presbyteries (all 113 voting for reunion) and 126 of 144 Old School presbyteries voting in the affirmative (with 15 presbyteries not reporting and 3 voting in the negative). Gutjahr, *Charles Hodge*, 341. Arguably, it was from this point that began what the renowned Princeton historian Lefferts A. Loetscher referred to as "the broadening [of the] church." See his book of that same title. A number of doctrinal trials followed, including those of Charles A. Briggs and Arthur C. McGiffert in the 1890s, two prominent professors of Old Testament and church history, respectively, at Union Theological Seminary in New York City, both tried for denying the inerrancy of Scripture and other perceived wrongs. See also Alan D. Strange, "The Legacy of Charles Hodge," in *Confident of Better Things: Essays Commemorating Seventy-Five Years of the Orthodox Presbyterian Church*, ed. John R. Muether and Danny E. Olinger (Willow Grove, PA: Committee for the Historian, 2011), 73–84.

church, by which he privileged doctrinal unity over political or any other sort of civil unity.

In the reunited church of 1869, and all that followed, the doctrine of the spirituality of the church had arguably been overwhelmed by the doctrine of "We all fought and died together in the war to preserve the Union and should be together in the church." The doctrine of the spirituality of the church gave way to unionism in state and church in the Northern Presbyterian Church: "waving the bloody shirt" of such unionism carried the day. Since the adoption of the Gardiner Spring Resolutions in 1861 and then during the war, the church had become more and more politicized, showing in the reunion of 1869 that the church was more interested in a unity based on things other than doctrine, which, for Hodge, spelled the decline of the church.

At the same time, the proponents of what Hodge regarded as an extreme spirituality of the church doctrine, rather than pulling the church back in a less politicized direction, probably only had the effect of pushing the church in a more politicized direction. Hodge had been a defender, and remained so until his death in 1878, of the spirituality of the church that saved the church from either extreme, from marginalization or politicization. Hodge's moderate approach and attempt to steer a careful and balanced course might still be of some value to us as we seek to relate the ecclesiastical to the social and political in our day.

6

The Spirituality of the Church
and Politics Today

CHARLES HODGE'S DOCTRINE of the spirituality of the church served to distinguish the church as an institution from other institutions, particularly the state, and to highlight that the mission of the church is a spiritual one. Since the church as a formal organization has nothing to do with politics as such—those specific matters of public policy that might divide persons who are otherwise in doctrinal accord—it does not address matters that are purely political. It is part of its proper spirituality and calling as a spiritual body having spiritual concerns, however, to address all that the Bible addresses, even if the underlying spiritual concerns have political ramifications.

Here's the rub: what is moral or ethical, and thus properly spiritual, cannot always readily be separated from what is "purely political." Moral issues—slavery being the primary example considered in this book—may have political ramifications: thus, what is "properly spiritual" and what may be "purely political" is not easily distinguished. One might wonder, then, if the doctrine of the spirituality of the church is essentially useless, dying the death of a thousand qualifications. I believe that it need not be: the principle that the church is a spiritual entity bearing spiritual concerns remains a valid consideration.

Every decision that the church as church takes needs to be justified in the light of the spirituality of the church, answering positively a question like "Does this advance the true spiritual task/calling/mission of the church?" Endorsing a political candidate and taking a position on a tax bill arguably does not pertain to or advance the cause of the gospel. Opposing American slavery, as did the 1818 General Assembly in its righteous statement calling for slavery's demise—without dictating precisely the political steps to end slavery—was arguably a proper concomitant of the gospel and the spirituality of the church.

Saying this, though, does not remove the difficulty of defining what is spiritual vis-à-vis what is more purely political. One man's "purely political" may be another man's "civil consequences of a proper spirituality." Nothing will save us from the debate over whether a matter pertains to the proper spirituality of the church or falls under the more purely political items that should not concern the church. And there are those on both left and right, particularly hard-liners, who see everything as political, so that all political issues are moral and all moral issues are purely political. Such partisans argue that every political issue is fraught with clear moral implications or, as Eric Metaxas claims, that the church need not fear being regarded as political but should, in fact, embrace it and readily address all sorts of political matters, even partisan ones that divide Christians.[1]

---

1   See especially his call for the church to "make sure that the will of the people is carried out." Eric Metaxas, *Letter to the American Church* (Washington, DC: Salem Books, 2022), 77.

Both ends of the spectrum involve ideologies that brook no distinctions (and thus no opposition), interested chiefly in the one to the exclusion of the many, tending toward absolutism and complete political domination. Whereas modernism crowned science, postmodernism has crowned politics, and everything has been politicized. In the wake of such pervasive politicization, Hodge's claim that one can distinguish the spiritual from the purely political itself becomes suspect. To one who regards everything as politics, Hodge's conviction that the church ought not to pursue purely political ends simply reflects a naive failure on his part to recognize how political all his convictions were. I would argue that where the line ought to be drawn between the spiritual and the political remains a challenge but that to deny a distinction can be made at all is to give way to a politicized cynicism.[2]

Many of the more conservative stripe express concerns about a politicizing church, about a church that is "woke" and lends too much support to forms of socialism. This is a valid concern. At the same time, the church should indeed sound a clear note about the unity of humanity, all being created in the image of God, and should teach that we are to love our neighbor without favoring the rich over the poor (James 2:1–13). To be concerned properly

---

The problems with this approach are legion, and I address them in a review of the book in both *New Horizons in the Orthodox Presbyterian Church*, May 2023, 21–22, and *Ordained Servant*, the journal for OPC officers: Alan D. Strange, "What Is the Primary Mission of the Church? A Review Article," *Ordained Servant* (January 2023).

2 James Davison Hunter has recognized the problem confronting "Christian transformation" both on the left and on the right and has suggested a third way, "faithful presence," that works itself out personally and institutionally in his challenging and provocative work *To Change the World: The Irony, Tragedy, and Possibility of Christianity in the Late Modern World* (New York: Oxford University Press, 2010). While the book has some significant weaknesses, its critique of an overly politicized church seems to hit the mark. An approach along these lines, though differing from Hunter in various aspects, might be consonant with a revival of a useful doctrine of the spirituality of the church.

for the poor and oppressed is not "wokeness" and Marxism. It is biblical. This does not mean, however, that the church should adopt a "woke" agenda as defined by outside agencies or advocate a particular economic system, like socialism.

It is one thing for Christians as individual Christians to argue, on the one hand, that free-market capitalism better coheres with biblical principles or, on the other hand, that a highly regulated market and some sort of state welfare, or socialism (a form of which is not antitheistic), does. Those are legitimate arguments among Christians. It is another thing for Christians of either stripe to argue that their view is what the Bible proclaims and thus what the institutional church should teach. The Bible does maintain private property and thus rules out "godless Communism" on this and other grounds. Socialism, however, manifests itself in several ways, some forms of which maintain private property and a market that retains some freedom, albeit under close governmental scrutiny. The point is not to argue for either of these but to argue that Christians may properly debate such topics.[3]

To be sure, some have thought that the Scriptures contain, if not a societal blueprint, something close to it. It is my conviction that neither the Old nor the New Testament contains all the details necessary to establish civil society.[4] Rather, particularly in the new covenant era, the matter of establishing a wise civil society is something to which Chris-

---

3 Douglas Wilson, in his new book *Mere Christendom* (Moscow, ID: Canon, 2023), seems to place what I regard as debatable political matters not explicitly addressed by the Bible (certainly not in detail) as beyond debate because (in his view) the Bible addresses them distinctly and clearly. See my review in upcoming issues of both *New Horizons and Mid-America Journal of Theology*.

4 As is sometimes noted, few things were more important in the ancient Near East than water rights, yet the Old Testament does not address them, testifying to the fact that civil law, even for Israel, always had aspects to it not coming directly from Scripture but developed from applying wisdom to the great command to love God and neighbor.

tians can well contribute, not because they have a detailed plan for it but because the principles of God's word are fitting both for doctrine and for life, needed as the basis for a just society, coming either directly from the Bible or indirectly through the works of the law written on the hearts of all (Rom. 2:13). Law abstracted from wisdom is never sufficient, as Job discovered from the counsel of his friends. Indeed, the Bible contains not only law but also other genres—certainly wisdom is a chief one—necessary for doctrine and life.

One may also note here, as we have from time to time in this work, that nothing I argue herein should ever be taken to mean that any area of life is not under God or that Christian faith is not all-comprehensive in its concerns. Many have capably addressed such matters, and a recent book that does so well is Bryan Chapell's *Grace at Work*, in which Chapell encourages Christians to live out their vocation or calling (butcher, baker, candlestick maker, as it were) consonant with the grace of God that has redeemed them.[5] Christians are not simply Sunday followers of Christ but those who serve all the time, "not by way of eye-service as people-pleasers, but with sincerity of heart, fearing the Lord." We are always in our Christian lives, and "whatever" we do, we are to do so "heartily, as for the Lord and not for men" (Col. 3:22–23).

The spirituality of the church rightly grasped and practiced should never be taken to mean that the whole of our Christian lives are not to be lived in faithful obedience to all that God has commanded, all to his glory, but rather that the church as church is a spiritual institution with a specific task, calling, and mission that should not be compromised by acting as if it were chiefly a political, social, or economic institution. We can attend both to

5 Bryan Chapell, *Grace at Work: Redeeming the Grind and the Glory of Your Job* (Wheaton, IL: Crossway, 2022).

the call to Christians to live the whole of their lives as Christians and to the call to the institutional church properly to be the church in distinction from other institutions like the family and the state.

Reprising Hodge

Charles Hodge distinguished the spiritual from the political as he did in a rather thoughtful way, even if one would disagree, as I do, with some of the decisions he made respecting slavery. Hodge refused to engage in some sort of precommitment that would box him in and not allow him to comment on something that some might deem more purely political but that he perceived as having clear spiritual ramifications. This can be seen in the way that Hodge responded to James Henley Thornwell's evocation of the spirituality of the church at the 1859 and 1860 General Assemblies. At those assemblies, Thornwell sought to shut down debate about agencies both external and internal to the church that he deemed a violation of the doctrine.

Hodge responded vigorously to Thornwell at the 1859 General Assembly, asserting, "There is a great temptation to adopt theories which free us from painful responsibilities."[6] Hodge characterized Thornwell's adducing of the spirituality of the church as such an attempt:

> To adopt any theory which would stop the mouth of the church, and prevent her bearing her testimony to the kings and rulers, magistrates and people, in behalf of the truth and law of God, is like one who administers chloroform to a man to prevent his doing mischief. We pray God that this poison

6 Charles Hodge, quoted in Strange, *Spirituality of the Church*, 259.

may be dashed away, before it has reduced the church to a state of inanition, and delivered her bound hand and foot into the power of the world.[7]

Hodge likewise opposed Thornwell's citation of the spirituality of the church at the 1860 General Assembly (when Thornwell argued against church boards), as well as those in Thornwell's line who argued similarly at the 1862 and 1865 General Assemblies, where Hodge's disputants defended a narrow doctrine that constructed as "political" what Hodge thought to be "spiritual."

Hodge's doctrine of the spirituality of the church was broader and more carefully constructed than that of Thornwell and his partisans, as seen in Hodge's opposition to the Gardiner Spring Resolutions at the 1861 General Assembly and his opposition to the pervasive politicization of the church reflected in the General Assemblies of the Civil War years and thereafter. Hodge, then, while critical of a narrowly constructed "superspiritual" view of the church, which considered the expression of any concern on the part of the church having civil consequences as inappropriate, also had and developed his own doctrine of the spirituality of the church. At bottom, though, Hodge and even his fiercest strict constructionist Old School Presbyterian opponents had more in common than dividing them—namely, they both taught, incautiously, that the Bible only regulated and never condemned slavery ipso facto and that the union of the American nation must continue. Hodge arguably moderated his own misgivings about slavery because he was convinced that to vent such might threaten the bonds that held the Presbyterian Church together,

---

7   Hodge, quoted in Strange, *Spirituality of the Church*, 260.

which would in turn threaten the bonds that held the American nation together.

It is arguable that Hodge, unlike the Covenanters, pulled his punches on slavery not only because of his own complicity with the institution but because for him, nothing was as important as the continuation of the American Union.[8] Even Thornwell, upon returning from Europe in 1860, proposed emancipation of the slaves to save the Union.[9] Why was such a premium placed on saving the American Union by so many of the parties in these debates? Hodge, Thornwell, and almost all those in nineteenth-century America shared certain convictions about American exceptionalism, namely, that God had brought the United States into existence to bring to the whole world both spiritual and political freedom.[10] All the parties to this dispute saw the American venture as divinely

8   Recent work on this question continues to highlight that, claims to the contrary notwith-standing, there was an important group—the British and American Covenanters—who both were confessionally orthodox and abolitionist, over against the common misconception that ardent opponents of slavery were either secularists or heterodox. See Daniel Ritchie, "Radical Orthodoxy: Irish Covenanters and American Slavery, circa 1830–1865," *Church History* 82, no. 4 (2013): 812–47. See also the more recent Joseph S. Moore, *Founding Sins: How a Group of Antislavery Radicals Fought to Put Christ into the Constitution* (New York: Oxford University Press, 2016).

9   And when it became clear that the Union could not be saved, Thornwell held that "the church is a spiritual institution *and* that the [Southern] confederacy ought to be explicitly Christian," as he had held for the Union earlier. What made possible his ability "to hold these two seemingly contradictory positions together coherently," as Christopher C. Cooper has argued, was that he continued to distinguish between "the church as an institution with a spiritual mission and Christianity as a religion that encompasses both institutions of church and state." Cooper, "Binding Bodies and Liberating Souls: James Henley Thornwell's Vision for a Spiritual Church and a Christian Confederacy," *Confessional Presbyterian* 9 (2013): 37.

10 This widespread conviction about American exceptionalism, particularly as held by Hodge and his fellow Old School Presbyterians, is intimated in Strange, *Spirituality of the Church*, chaps. 5–7, but much more explicitly documented and exposited in Mark A. Noll, *America's God: From Jonathan Edwards to Abraham Lincoln* (New York: Oxford University Press, 2002), esp. 227–364, where Noll develops how "American ideologies exerted a profound impact on religion." For a helpful discussion of this whole matter, see John D. Wilsey, *American*

ordained and worth saving at all costs, even if that meant bearing with the continuation of slavery, which Hodge and the 1818 General Assembly said should end.

This commitment to the American experiment, though cast in spiritual terms, was a political commitment, and abolitionism threatened the continuation of the holy "errand into the wilderness" that Hodge and others saw the American nation to be. Hence, even if slavery was undesirable, as Hodge thought it was and thus advocated gradual emancipation, slavery was not horrible enough for Hodge to warrant its abolition, certainly not at the price of the dissolution of the nation. Thus, for Hodge, Thornwell, and most Presbyterians, Old and New School alike, the survival of the nation transcended all other concerns and was itself conceived not merely as a political conviction but as a spiritual truism since the continued existence of the nation was a precondition of the continued existence and thriving of the American Presbyterian Church. All the parties to this thinking were so enmeshed in their political commitments to the US Constitution that the continuing union of the American nation was sacrosanct and beyond question. For Hodge and his fellows, nothing rose to the moral level of supporting the survival of the nation. The continuation of the Union became paramount to every other consideration.

There was then a kind of "spiritualized" manifest destiny that arguably ran quite counter to any vigorous notion of the spirituality of the church. Hodge, Thornwell, and all the rest, New or Old School, looked for the blessings that had come to the American nation to come to the world through America; thus, the American nation had to spread and be preserved at all costs for the good of the propagation

_____

Exceptionalism and Civil Religion: Reassessing the History of an Idea (Downers Grove, IL: IVP Academic, 2015).

of the Christian faith everywhere. They were in effect identifying the United States with the church as the means of worldwide blessing. Perhaps this pervasive spiritual imperialism means that the spirituality of the church is a chimera and that time-and-space-located parishioners are always more influenced by political concerns than they realize or would ever wish to acknowledge. Some might argue that since politics is inescapable and cannot in any case be easily distinguished from matters spiritual (the political simply being an expression of the moral or spiritual), one ought not even try to distinguish them, and we would best be done with all this talk about the spirituality of the church.

But the politicization of everything, including the church, and a denial of the spirituality of the church as either Hodge or Thornwell conceived it together render the church just one more voice among the many pushing a political agenda. The church, particularly as set forth on the pages of the New Testament, does not appear to be anything of the sort. The church is not presented in the Bible as simply another voice in the competing cacophony of shouted slogans but rather that still small voice that testifies to what God has done for us in Christ, that he so loved the world that he gave Christ to die for it, so that all who believe in him should not perish but have everlasting life (John 3:16). This is the message of the church, and to reduce it to a mere political agenda is to sell short the glory of the gospel. The Christian faith is not, at its heart, a political message but a spiritual one. A doctrine of the spirituality of the church, properly conceived, holds fast to this thrust and permits the church to maintain fidelity to the Christian message while keeping in check any address that it might consider necessary respecting matters in the civil and political sphere.

Scripture and Slavery

Part of the problem in the American Presbyterian Church with respect to the slavery question had to do with the fact that many in the church thought that Scripture did not appear to be opposed to slavery but only sought to regulate it. Hodge had difficulty getting beyond the contention that the Scriptures did not forbid slavery outright, and thus he assumed that the church should not either. I think that he simply missed that the Scriptures did forbid Hebrews from enslaving each other and allowed it only for strangers as a mercy to some whom the Israelites were otherwise commanded to kill. The church was not given such a commission (to eliminate certain nations) but to preach the gospel to the whole world. While it is true that Christ and the apostles did not abolish slavery, it is also the case that the consequences of the gospel would tend to ameliorate if not eliminate it (seen in Paul's letter to Philemon).[11]

Had Christ or Paul ordered the end of all slavery, it would have rendered the gospel revolutionary and made its central concern social, political, and economic equity. If Paul, for instance, had simply commanded Philemon to free Onesimus and not suggested that he be emancipated as a consequence of the new relationship that they sustained in the gospel, Christians would have viewed such an apostolic command as binding, necessitating the abolition of slavery immediately everywhere. This would have obscured the

---

11 This trajectory is seen in the practices of Christians in the early church, as described in J. Albert Harrill, *The Manumission of Slaves in Early Christianity* (Tübingen: Mohr Siebeck, 1995). Opposition to slavery itself, in contrast with merely slavery's abuses, was long in coming, as seen in Trevor Dennis, "Man beyond Price: St. Gregory of Nyssa and Slavery," in *Heaven and Earth: Essex Essays in Theology and Ethics*, ed. Andrew Linzey and Peter J. Wexler (Worthing, West Sussex, UK: Churchman, 1986). Nonetheless, it was Christianity, or Christendom, at least in part, that brought slavery to an effective end between the fourth and tenth centuries, with serfdom developing in seignorialism and feudalism rising after slavery's diminution.

true spiritual message of the gospel—salvation in Christ to all who believe in him—and would have boiled down the Christian faith to another competing—indeed, radical—political agenda, especially in the Greco-Roman world, where so much of the population was in slavery. This would have rendered Christianity, which is truly revolutionary in terms of its proclamation of the Christ, another merely political revolutionary movement. Christ was not the Vladimir Lenin or Che Guevara of his time but the Lamb of God who takes away the sin of the world. The New Testament contains no explicit commands to abolish slavery, though it prohibits manstealing (1 Tim. 1:10) and thus proscribes the form of slavery that was practiced in the United States; rather, the New Testament left the ending of slavery to the *outworking* of the gospel in the Greco-Roman world of its day.[12]

The American Legacy of the Spirituality Doctrine

In the American context, developments during and after the US Civil War arguably justified Hodge's contention that there was a proper spiritual-political distinction to be made with respect to matters ecclesiastical. Not only was the Old School Presbyterian Church unduly politicized during the war, so that civil concerns routinely eclipsed theological ones, but also after the reunion of the Old and New School in the North, the Presbyterian Church, along with other mainstream Protestant churches, seemed more committed and motivated by political

---

12 Though Kyle Harper, in *Slavery in the Late Roman World, AD 275–425* (New York: Cambridge University Press, 2011), shows that slavery lasted deep into the Christian era, in his more recent book, *From Shame to Sin: The Christian Transformation of Sexual Morality in Late Antiquity* (Cambridge, MA: Harvard University Press, 2013), he shows that Christianity's strict moral code was particularly sympathetic to the slave who had been sexually exploited. So Christianity played an important role in reforming and ultimately ending ancient slavery.

than religious concerns. Civil religion, in other words, became more and more the order of the day in the twentieth century for the American Protestant church, and the engine of social concerns drove the Presbyterian Church more than did the Bible or the Westminster Standards.[13]

Woodrow Wilson was the first Southerner after the Civil War—and was also a Presbyterian—who became president of the United States, coming from a rich heritage of the spirituality of the church (his father, Joseph Ruggles Wilson, became the stated clerk of the PCCSA [later PCUS], the Southern Old School Presbyterian Church, at its formation in 1861). Woodrow Wilson, however, completely rejected the spirituality of the church, thoroughly identifying the religious and the political, particularly baptizing his own political ideals and investing them with the authority of divine sanction.[14] Wilson scarcely distinguished his own programs from sacred writ, true also of Theodore Roosevelt and many politicians of the time.[15] In this way, these men and many others who followed

---

13 This is why Ernest Trice Thompson so vigorously opposed the doctrine of the spirituality of the church. He did indeed oppose the doctrine because it had been used in support of slavery and was afterward used to justify repressive racial policies, but he also opposed it because he supported the church playing a larger and more direct political role in civil society. See his *Spirituality of the Church: A Distinctive Doctrine of the Presbyterian Church in the United States* (Richmond, VA: John Knox, 1961).

14 A. Scott Berg, *Wilson* (New York: G. P. Putnam's Sons, 2013). In this remarkable work, Berg shows the almost complete identification in Woodrow Wilson of his politics with his religion, with every chapter title reflecting Wilson's near-messianic sensibilities ("Advent," "Baptism," "Gethsemane," "Passion," and so forth).

15 Made abundantly clear in Edmund Morris's three-volume work on Roosevelt: *The Rise of Theodore Roosevelt*, rev. ed. (New York: Random House, 2001); *Theodore Rex* (New York: Random House, 2001); *Colonel Roosevelt* (New York: Random House, 2010). Also shown in Doris Kearns Goodwin, *The Bully Pulpit: Theodore Roosevelt, William Howard Taft, and the Golden Age of Journalism* (New York: Simon & Schuster, 2013). Roosevelt was a long-time member of the Reformed Church in America (RCA), a close cousin of the Presbyterian Church in the United States of America (PCUSA).

them compromised the spiritual independence of the church and put it in the service of their political programs.

The purpose of the church, however, is not to serve such lesser ends. Ultimately, to evoke Calvin's thought, the church is a spiritual hospital dispensing medicine for needy, sin-sick souls. The church's essential spiritual character was, for Hodge, central to his doctrine of the spirituality of the church. Yes, spirituality meant that the church had a certain province and certain boundaries that distinguished it from other institutions, particularly the state. It meant that the church was to be the church and not seek merely to imitate the world. What marked the church off from every other institution was that it was the body created and possessed by the Holy Spirit. Hodge's doctrine of the spirituality of the church, then, was not merely a concomitant of his polity but came out of the heart of his theology. Hodge, like Calvin, was a theologian of the Holy Spirit, and this, above all, informed his doctrine of the spirituality of the church.

Did Hodge and others of the Old School Presbyterian Church, however, properly apply this doctrine when they refused to condemn American slavery consistently, in both theory and practice? Or is the doctrine of the spirituality of the church fatally flawed, containing the seeds of its own destruction by limiting and marginalizing the church? In whatever way one answers these questions, it is certainly true that the American Presbyterian Church, particularly in its Old School form, never lived up to the vigorous denunciation of slavery issued by the 1818 General Assembly. That assembly called American chattel slavery a failure to love one's neighbor and a scourge on a society composed largely of Christians. It argued for the extirpation of slavery and the emancipation of slaves.

But the swirling events of the following years seemed to wipe away that clarion call, and slavery became more entrenched than ever and practically untouchable. The 1845 General Assembly, and Hodge agreed with it, saw slavery as an issue so divisive that it would destroy the union of the church and the nation. That anyone ever used the spirituality of the church in any of its forms to refrain from such moral rejection of slavery is greatly lamentable.

We must understand the spirituality of the church in its nineteenth-century American context, as I have sought to do in this book, since that is the time when this concept was fully developed. We must judge both its strengths and weaknesses in that context before we can talk about a "usable" doctrine of the spirituality of the church in our time. We need to assess how the church has abused this doctrine in the past as well as how it has beneficially used it if we are to employ it in any helpful way now and in the future.

Christians Engaging the World

The spirituality of the church, properly, does not mean, and must not mean, either that the institutional church or Christians fail to care for the world around them. In the great tsunami of 2004, Christians, Christian organizations, and Christian churches responded with overwhelming aid. Hindus and Muslims, because of their different theological convictions, tended not to, viewing the destruction as deserved karma or the wrath of Allah against bad Muslims. Christians must never respond in this way but must respond with the compassion and self-sacrifice that befits followers of Jesus.

The spirituality of the church ought not to prompt us to say, "Be warmed, be filled, and go away." It frees us to serve God and each other. It does not make us those who flee the world but those who are able to engage each other from the best vantage point, as

Princeton professor B. B. Warfield noted in his masterful sermon "Imitating the Incarnation":

> Self-sacrifice brought Christ into the world. And self-sacrifice will lead us, His followers, not away from but into the midst of men. Wherever men suffer, there will we be to comfort. Wherever men strive, there will we be to help. Wherever men fail, there will we be to uplift. Wherever men succeed, there will we be to rejoice. Self-sacrifice means not indifference to our times and our fellows: it means absorption in them. It means forgetfulness of self in others. It means entering into every man's hopes and fears, longings and despairs: it means many-sidedness of spirit, multiform activity, multiplicity of sympathies. It means richness of development. It means not that we should live one life, but a thousand lives—binding ourselves to a thousand souls by the filaments of so loving a sympathy that their lives become ours. It means that all the experiences of men shall smite our souls and shall beat and batter these stubborn hearts of ours into fitness for their heavenly home.[16]

While it is right that the spirituality of the church prompts us to remember the task and calling of the church—to gather and perfect the saints by the means of grace empowered by the Holy Spirit—we must not forget that the mission of the church is always accompanied by and integrally involves good works, love for God and our fellow man. The church as an institution both preaches the gospel to all people and shows the manifold love of God to all people by offering a cup of cold water in Christ's name.

---

16 B. B. Warfield, "Imitating the Incarnation," in *The Person and Work of Christ* (1914; repr., Phillipsburg, NJ: Presbyterian and Reformed, 1970), 574–75.

The spiritual independence of the church—the doctrine of the spirituality of the church—should never be taken to mean that the church may attend to its religious duties and fail to love its neighbor. Like the good Samaritan, we must seek to be a good neighbor even to those whom we would rather ignore and not help. We must seek both to preach the gospel and to do good to all people, especially those of the household of faith (Gal. 6:10). Not only is such a holistic approach not at variance with the spirituality of the church, but it is part of a proper living out of the spirituality of the church.

I think that the reintroduction of this doctrine into present theological conversations can have a salubrious effect but only if we embrace what is at its heart, true spirituality, and reject its bad by-products, apathy to our world and its needs. We must not allow a simple claim that something violates the spirituality of the church to settle a matter. We must not imagine that a mere citation of "the spirituality of the church" disposes of problems, allowing us to conveniently dismiss difficult matters, dispensing with the hard work of looking carefully at all that comes before us. Rather, we should look at every proposal on its own terms and thoughtfully apply the principle of the spirituality of the church. The spirituality of the church then could be recovered for the ongoing dialogue of how the church is to relate to the world in which it finds itself, both in how it distinguishes itself from the world and how it gives itself to the world.

Bibliography

Manuscripts by Charles Hodge

The Department of Archives and Special Collections at the Speer and Luce Libraries of Princeton Theological Seminary, Princeton, New Jersey, houses the single largest collection of Hodge's manuscripts, consisting of forty-seven archival boxes (17.8 linear feet). Items cited from this collection are referred to as belonging to the Charles Hodge Manuscript Collection (CHMC).

The Department of Rare Books and Special Collections at the Princeton University Library, Princeton, New Jersey, holds a collection consisting of twenty-seven archival boxes (13.5 linear feet) that contains the personal papers of Hodge, including lectures, speeches, articles, books, and correspondence dealing with questions of Presbyterian theology in the mid- to late nineteenth century. Items cited from this collection are referred to as belonging to the Charles Hodge Papers (CHP).

Published Works and Dissertations

Augustine. *The City of God against the Pagans*. Translated and edited by R. W. Dyson. New York: Cambridge University Press, 1998.

Baird, Samuel J. *A Collection of the Acts, Deliverances, and Testimonies of the Supreme Judicatory of the Presbyterian Church.* Philadelphia: Presbyterian Board of Publications, 1855.

Beeke, Jonathon D. *Duplex Regnum Christi: Christ's Twofold Kingdom in Reformed Theology.* Leiden: Brill, 2021.

Berg, A. Scott. *Wilson.* New York: G. P. Putnam's Sons, 2013.

Beringer, Richard E., Herman Hattaway, Archer Jones, and William N. Still Jr. *Why the South Lost the Civil War.* Athens: University of Georgia Press, 1986.

The Book of Church Order of the Orthodox Presbyterian Church. Willow Grove, PA: Committee on Christian Education of the Orthodox Presbyterian Church, 2020.

The Book of Church Order of the Presbyterian Church in America. Atlanta: The Office of the Stated Clerk of the General Assembly of the Presbyterian Church in America, 2022.

Bourne, George. *Man-Stealing and Slavery Denounced by the Presbyterian and Methodist Churches, Together with an Address to All the Churches.* Boston: Garrison & Knapp, 1834.

Brown, Guy Story. *Calhoun's Philosophy of Politics: A Study of "A Disquisition on Government."* Macon, GA: Mercer University Press, 2000.

Burin, Eric. *Slavery and the Peculiar Solution: A History of the American Colonization Society.* Gainesville: University of Florida Press, 2005.

Calvin, John. *Institutes of the Christian Religion.* Edited by John T. McNeill. Translated by Ford Lewis Battles. Library of Christian Classics. Philadelphia: Westminster, 1960.

Carson, D. A. *Christ and Culture Revisited.* Grand Rapids, MI: Eerdmans, 2008.

Carter, Craig A. *Rethinking Christ and Culture: A Post-Christendom Perspective.* Grand Rapids, MI: Brazos, 2006.

Carwardine, Richard J. "The Politics of Charles Hodge." In *Charles Hodge Revisited: A Critical Appraisal of His Life and Work*, edited by John W. Stewart and James H. Moorhead, 247–97. Grand Rapids, MI: Eerdmans, 2002.

Chan, Simon. *Spiritual Theology: A Systematic Study of the Christian Life*. Downers Grove, IL: InterVarsity Press, 1998.

Chapell, Bryan. *Grace at Work: Redeeming the Grind and the Glory of Your Job*. Wheaton, IL: Crossway, 2022.

Chesebrough, David B. *Clergy Dissent in the Old South, 1830–1865*. Carbondale: Southern Illinois University Press, 1996.

Chesebrough, David B., ed. *"God Ordained This War": Sermons on the Sectional Crisis, 1830–1865*. Columbia: University of South Carolina Press, 1991.

Church of Scotland. *The First and Second Books of Discipline*. 1560 and 1578. Reprint, Dallas: Presbyterian Heritage Publications, 1993.

Cooper, Christopher C. "Binding Bodies and Liberating Souls: James Henley Thornwell's Vision for a Spiritual Church and a Christian Confederacy." *Confessional Presbyterian* 9 (2013): 35–47.

Cousins, Ewert, gen. ed. *World Spirituality: An Encyclopedic History of the Religious Quest*. New York: Crossroad, 1985–.

Davis, David Brion. *Inhuman Bondage: The Rise and Fall of Slavery in the New World*. New York: Oxford, 2006.

Davis, David Brion. *In the Image of God: Religion, Moral Values, and Our Heritage of Slavery*. New Haven, CT: Yale University Press, 2001.

Davis, David Brion. *The Problem of Slavery in Western Culture*. Ithaca, NY: Cornell University Press, 1966.

Degler, Carl N. *The Other South: Southern Dissenters in the Nineteenth Century*. New York: Harper and Row, 1974.

Dew, Charles B. *Apostles of Disunion: Southern Secession Commissioners and the Causes of the Civil War*. Charlottesville: University of Virginia Press, 2002.

DeYoung, Kevin. "The Rise of Right-Wing Wokeism—Review: *The Case for Christian Nationalism* by Stephen Wolfe." The Gospel Coalition, November 28, 2022. https://www.thegospelcoalition.org/.

DeYoung, Kevin, and Greg Gilbert. *What Is the Mission of the Church? Making Sense of Social Justice, Shalom, and the Great Commission*. Wheaton, IL: Crossway, 2011.

Elliott, E. N., ed. *Cotton Is King, and Pro-Slavery Arguments: Comprising the Writings of Hammond, Harper, Christy, Stringfellow, Hodge, Bledsoe, and Cartwright, on This Important Subject*. Augusta, GA: Pritchard, Abbott & Loomis, 1860.

Estelle, Bryan D. *The Primary Mission of the Church: Engaging or Transforming the World?* Fearn, Ross-shire, Scotland: Mentor, 2022.

Evans, Christopher H. *The Social Gospel in American Religion: A History*. New York: New York University Press, 2017.

Farmer, James O., Jr. *The Metaphysical Confederacy: James Henley Thornwell and the Synthesis of Southern Values*. Macon, GA: Mercer University Press, 1986.

Faust, Drew Gilpin, ed. *The Ideology of Slavery: Proslavery Thought in the Antebellum South, 1830–1860*. Baton Rouge: Louisiana State University Press, 1981.

Fogel, Robert William, and Stanley L. Engerman. *Time on the Cross: The Economics of American Negro Slavery*. New York: Little Brown, 1974.

Ford, Lacy K. *Deliver Us from Evil: The Slavery Question in the Old South*. New York: Oxford University Press, 2009.

Freehling, William W. "James Henley Thornwell's Mysterious Antislavery Moment." *Journal of Southern History* 57, no. 3 (1991): 383–406.

Goen, C. C. *Broken Churches, Broken Nation: Denominational Schisms and the Coming of the Civil War*. Macon, GA: Mercer University Press, 1985.

Goodwin, Doris Kearns. *The Bully Pulpit: Theodore Roosevelt, William Howard Taft, and the Golden Age of Journalism*. New York: Simon & Schuster, 2013.

Graham, Preston D., Jr. *A Kingdom Not of This World: Stuart Robinson's Struggle to Distinguish the Sacred from the Secular during the American Civil War*. Macon, GA: Mercer University Press, 2002.

Guelzo, Allen C. *Abraham Lincoln: Redeemer President*. Grand Rapids, MI: Eerdmans, 1999.

Gutjahr, Paul C. *Charles Hodge: Guardian of American Orthodoxy*. New York: Oxford University Press, 2011.

Harper, Kyle. *From Shame to Sin: The Christian Transformation of Sexual Morality in Late Antiquity*. Cambridge, MA: Harvard University Press, 2013.

Harper, Kyle. *Slavery in the Late Roman World, AD 275–425*. New York: Cambridge University Press, 2011.

Harrill, J. Albert. *The Manumission of Slaves in Early Christianity*. Tübingen: Mohr Siebeck, 1995.

Hart, Darryl. *A Secular Faith: Why Christianity Favors the Separation of Church and State*. Chicago: Ivan Dee, 2006.

Hart, D. G., and John R. Muether. *Seeking a Better Country: 300 Years of American Presbyterianism*. Phillipsburg, NJ: P&R, 2007.

Hart, D. G., and John R. Muether. "The Spirituality of the Church." *Ordained Servant* 7, no. 3 (1998): 64–66.

Hewison, J. K. *The Covenanters: A History of the Church in Scotland from the Reformation to the Revolution*. 2 vols. 1913. Reprint, Edinburgh: Banner of Truth, 2019.

Hodge, A. A. *The Life of Charles Hodge, D.D., LL.D.* New York: Charles Scribner's Sons, 1880.

Hodge, Charles. *Discussions in Church Polity.* 1878. Reprint, New York: Westminster, 2001.

Hodge, Charles. Select articles. *Biblical Repertory* (Princeton, NJ, 1825–1829); *Biblical Repertory and Theological Review* (Princeton, NJ, 1830–1836); *Biblical Repertory and Princeton Review* (Princeton, NJ: College of New Jersey, 1837–1871).

Hoffecker, W. Andrew. *Charles Hodge: The Pride of Princeton.* Phillipsburg, NJ: P&R, 2011.

Holifield, E. Brooks. *The Gentleman Theologians: American Theology in Southern Culture, 1795–1860.* Durham, NC: Duke University Press, 1978.

Howe, Daniel Walker. *What Hath God Wrought: The Transformation of America, 1815–1848.* Oxford History of the United States. New York: Oxford University Press, 2007.

Hunter, James Davison. *To Change the World: The Irony, Tragedy, and Possibility of Christianity in the Late Modern World.* New York: Oxford University Press, 2010.

Innes, David C. *Christ and the Kingdoms of Men: Foundations of Political Life.* Phillipsburg, NJ: P&R, 2019.

Irons, Charles F. *The Origins of Proslavery Christianity: White and Black Evangelicals in Colonial and Antebellum Virginia.* Chapel Hill: University of North Carolina Press, 2008.

Kaemingk, Matthew, ed. *Reformed Public Theology: A Global Vision for Life in the World.* Grand Rapids, MI: Baker Academic, 2021.

Keller, Timothy. *Center Church: Doing Balanced, Gospel-Centered Ministry in Your City.* Grand Rapids, MI: Zondervan, 2012.

Kuyper, Abraham. *Collected Works in Public Theology.* Vol. 3, *Common Grace: God's Gifts for a Fallen World.* 1904. Edited by Jordan J. Ballor and J. Daryl Charles. Translated by Nelson D. Kloosterman and Ed M. van der Maas. Bellingham, WA: Lexham, 2020.

Leeman, Jonathan. *Political Church: The Local Assembly as Embassy of Christ's Rule.* Downers Grove, IL: IVP Academic, 2016.

Loetscher, Lefferts A. *A Brief History of the Presbyterians.* 4th ed. Philadelphia: Westminster, 1983.

Loetscher, Lefferts A. *The Broadening Church: A Study of Theological Issues in the Presbyterian Church since 1869.* Philadelphia: University of Pennsylvania Press, 1954.

Lucas, Sean Michael. *For a Continuing Church: The Roots of the Presbyterian Church in America.* Phillipsburg, NJ: P&R, 2015.

Machen, J. Gresham. *Christianity and Liberalism.* 1923. Reprint, Grand Rapids, MI: Eerdmans, 1994.

Maddex, Jack P. "From Theocracy to Spirituality: The Southern Presbyterian Reversal on Church and State." *Journal of Presbyterian History* 54, no. 4 (1976): 438–57.

Mayse, Edgar Caldwell. "Robert Jefferson Breckinridge: American Presbyterian Controversialist." PhD diss., Union Theological Seminary, 1974.

McGinn, Bernard. *Christian Spirituality.* New York: Crossroad, 1987.

McGinn, Bernard. *Foundations of Mysticism.* New York: Crossroad, 1995.

McIlhenny, Ryan C. *To Preach Deliverance to the Captives: Freedom and Slavery in the Protestant Mind of George Bourne, 1780–1845.* Baton Rouge: Louisiana State University Press, 2020.

McLeod, Alexander. *Negro Slavery Unjustifiable: A Discourse.* New York: T. & J. Swords, 1802.

McPherson, James. *Battle Cry of Freedom: The Civil War Era.* Oxford History of the United States. New York: Oxford University Press, 2003.

Metaxas, Eric. *Letter to the American Church.* Washington, DC: Salem Books, 2022.

Minutes of the General Assembly of the Presbyterian Church in the United States of America (select volumes). Philadelphia: Presbyterian Board of Publications, 1838–1869.

Minutes of the General Assembly of the Presbyterian Church in the United States of America from Its Organization, A.D. 1789–A.D. 1820. Philadelphia: Presbyterian Board of Publications, 1847.

Moore, Joseph S. *Founding Sins: How a Group of Antislavery Radicals Fought to Put Christ into the Constitution.* New York: Oxford University Press, 2016.

Morgan, Edmund S. *American Slavery, American Freedom.* New York: Norton, 1975.

Morris, Edmund. *Colonel Roosevelt.* New York: Random House, 2010.

Morris, Edmund. *The Rise of Theodore Roosevelt.* Rev. ed. New York: Random House, 2001.

Morris, Edmund. *Theodore Rex.* New York: Random House, 2001.

Murchie, David Neil. "Morality and Social Ethics in the Thought of Charles Hodge." PhD diss., Drew University, 1980.

Niebuhr, H. Richard. *Christ and Culture.* New York: Harper and Brothers, 1951.

Noll, Mark A. *America's God: From Jonathan Edwards to Abraham Lincoln.* New York: Oxford University Press, 2002.

Noll, Mark A. *The Civil War as a Theological Crisis.* Chapel Hill: University of North Carolina Press, 2006.

O'Donovan, Oliver. *The Desire of the Nations: Rediscovering the Roots of Political Theology.* New York: Cambridge University Press, 1996.

Ouweneel, Willem J. *The World Is Christ's: A Critique of Two Kingdoms Theology.* Toronto: Ezra Press, 2017.

Potter, David M. *The Impending Crisis, 1848–1861.* New York: Harper and Row, 1976.

Rian, Edwin H. *The Presbyterian Conflict*. Grand Rapids, MI: Eerdmans, 1940.

Ritchie, Daniel. "Radical Orthodoxy: Irish Covenanters and American Slavery, circa 1830–1865." *Church History* 82, no. 4 (2013): 812–47.

Robinson, Stuart. *The Church of God as an Essential Element of the Gospel, and the Idea, Structure, and Functions Thereof*. Philadelphia: Joseph M. Wilson, 1858.

Robinson, Stuart. *Slavery as Recognized in the Mosaic Civil Law, and as Recognized Also, and Allowed, in the Abrahamic, Mosaic, and Christian Church*. Toronto: Rollo & Adam, 1865.

Smith, Morton H. *How Is the Gold Become Dim: The Decline of the Presbyterian Church, U.S., as Reflected in Its Assembly Actions*. Jackson, MS: Premier, 1973.

Spangler, Jewel L. "Proslavery Presbyterians: Virginia's Conservative Dissenters in the Age of Revolution." *Journal of Presbyterian History* 78, no. 2 (2000): 111–23.

Stampp, Kenneth M. *The Peculiar Institution: Slavery in the Antebellum South*. New York: Knopf, 1956.

Steers, Edward, Jr. *Blood on the Moon: The Assassination of Abraham Lincoln*. Lexington: University of Kentucky Press, 2001.

Stewart, John. "Charles Hodge as a Public Theologian." In *Theology as Conversation: The Significance of Dialogue in Historical and Contemporary Theology; A Festschrift for Daniel L. Migliore*, edited by Bruce L. McCormack and Kimlyn J. Bender, 341–60. Grand Rapids, MI: Eerdmans, 2009.

Stout, Harry S. *Upon the Altar of the Nation: A Moral History of the Civil War*. New York: Viking, 2006.

Strange, Alan D. "Charles Hodge on Office and the Nature of Presbyterianism." In *Charles Hodge: American Orthodox Reformed*

Theologian, edited by Ryan M. McGraw, 231–65. Leiden: Vandenhoeck and Ruprecht, 2023.

Strange, Alan D. "Church and State in Historical Perspective." *Ordained Servant* 16 (2007): 93–100.

Strange, Alan D. "Commentary on the Form of Government of the Orthodox Presbyterian Church" and "Commentary on the Book of Discipline of the Orthodox Presbyterian Church." In *Ordained Servant Online* (April 2020–ongoing). https://www.opc.org/os.html.

Strange, Alan D. *The Doctrine of the Spirituality of the Church in the Ecclesiology of Charles Hodge*. Reformed Academic Dissertations. Phillipsburg, NJ: P&R, 2017.

Strange, Alan D. "The Legacy of Charles Hodge." In *Confident of Better Things: Essays Commemorating Seventy-Five Years of the Orthodox Presbyterian Church*, edited by John R. Muether and Danny E. Olinger, 73–84. Willow Grove, PA: Committee for the Historian, 2011.

Strange, Alan D. "2001 Preface to Charles Hodge's *The Church and Its Polity*." *Mid-America Journal of Theology* 13 (2002): 25–37.

Tatum, Georgia Lee. *Disloyalty in the Confederacy*. 1934. Reprint, Whitefish, MT: Literary Licensing, 2011.

Thompson, Ernest Trice. *Presbyterians in the South*. 3 vols. Richmond, VA: John Knox, 1963–1973.

Thompson, Ernest Trice. *The Spirituality of the Church: A Distinctive Doctrine of the Presbyterian Church in the United States*. Richmond, VA: John Knox, 1961.

Thornwell, James Henley. *Collected Writings*. Vol. 4. 1875. Reprint, Carlisle, PA: Banner of Truth, 1974.

Tisby, Jemar. *The Color of Compromise: The Truth about the American Church's Complicity in Racism*. Grand Rapids, MI: Zondervan, 2019.

Tisby, Jemar. *How to Fight Racism: Courageous Christianity and the Journey toward Racial Justice*. Grand Rapids, MI: Zondervan Reflective, 2021.

Tise, Larry. *A History of the Defense of Slavery in America, 1701–1840*. Athens: University of Georgia Press, 1990.

Torbett, David. *Theology and Slavery: Charles Hodge and Horace Bushnell*. Macon, GA: Mercer University Press, 2006.

Troxel, A. Craig. Foreword to *The Church of God as an Essential Element of the Gospel*, by Stuart Robinson, 5–12. 1858. Reprint, Willow Grove, PA: Committee on Christian Education of the Orthodox Presbyterian Church, 2009.

Trueman, Carl R. *The Rise and Triumph of the Modern Self: Cultural Amnesia, Expressive Individualism, and the Road to Sexual Revolution*. Wheaton, IL: Crossway, 2020.

Vander Velde, Lewis G. *The Presbyterian Churches and the Federal Union, 1861–1869*. Cambridge, MA: Harvard University Press, 1932.

VanDrunen, David. *Living in God's Two Kingdoms: A Biblical Vision for Christianity and Culture*. Wheaton, IL: Crossway, 2010.

VanDrunen, David. *Natural Law and the Two Kingdoms: A Study in the Development of Reformed Social Thought*. Grand Rapids, MI: Eerdmans, 2010.

VanDrunen, David. *Politics after Christendom: Political Theology in a Fractured World*. Grand Rapids, MI: Zondervan Academic, 2020.

Volf, Miroslav. *Exclusion and Embrace: A Theological Exploration of Identity, Otherness, and Reconciliation*. Nashville: Abingdon, 1996.

Volf, Miroslav. *Flourishing: Why We Need Religion in a Globalized World*. New Haven, CT: Yale University Press, 2015.

Wallace, Peter J. "'The Bond of Union': The Old School Presbyterian Church and the American Nation, 1837–1861." PhD diss., University of Notre Dame, 2004.

Warfield, B. B. "Imitating the Incarnation." In *The Person and Work of Christ*. 1914. Reprint, Phillipsburg, NJ: Presbyterian and Reformed, 1970.

Waters, Guy Prentiss. *How Jesus Runs the Church*. Phillipsburg, NJ: P&R, 2011.

Watson, Philip S. *Let God Be God! An Interpretation of the Theology of Martin Luther*. Philadelphia: Muhlenberg, 1949.

Westminster Confession of Faith and Catechisms as Adopted by the Orthodox Presbyterian Church. Willow Grove, PA: Committee on Christian Education of the Orthodox Presbyterian Church, 2005.

White, Ronald C. "Lincoln's Sermon on the Mount: The Second Inaugural." In *Religion and the American Civil War*, edited by Randall M. Miller, Harry S. Stout, and Charles Reagan Wilson, 208–25. New York: Oxford University Press, 1998.

Whitehead, Andrew L., and Samuel L. Perry. *Taking America Back for God: Christian Nationalism in the United States*. New York: Oxford University Press, 2020.

Whitford, David M. *The Curse of Ham in the Early Modern Era: The Bible and the Justifications for Slavery*. Burlington, VT: Ashgate, 2009.

Wilentz, Sean. *The Rise of American Democracy: Jefferson to Lincoln*. New York: Norton, 2005.

Willson, James Renwick. *Political Danger: Essays on the Mediatorial Kingship of Christ over Nations and Their Political Institutions, 1809–1838*. Pittsburgh: Crown and Covenant, 2009.

Wilsey, John D. *American Exceptionalism and Civil Religion: Reassessing the History of an Idea*. Downers Grove, IL: IVP Academic, 2015.

Wingard, Brian T. "'As the Lord Puts Words in Her Mouth': The Supremacy of Scripture in the Ecclesiology of James Henley Thornwell and Its Influence upon the Presbyterian Churches of the South." PhD diss., Westminster Theological Seminary, 1992.

Wolfe, Stephen. *The Case for Christian Nationalism.* Moscow, ID: Canon, 2022.

Wood, Gordon S. *Empire of Liberty: A History of the Early Republic, 1789–1815.* Oxford History of the United States. New York: Oxford University Press, 2009.

General Index

abolitionism, 32–35, 73, 118n8
abusus non tollit usum, 13n19
Address to All Churches of Christ
(PCCSA), xi
African colonization, 45
Alexander, Archibald, 45n39
American Colonization Society, 45n39
American exceptionalism, 118–19
American freedom, built on back of
American slavery, 35
Anglican Church, bond of union of,
107
Arminianism, 107n57
Augustine, 9–10

Baird, Samuel J., 37n16
Beeke, Jonathon, 19
Berg, A. Scott, 123n14
Beringer, Richard E., 76n22
Bible
infallibility of, 33n5
on slavery, 32, 34, 49, 117, 121–22
Biblical Repertory and Princeton Review,
22, 55–56
Boardman, Henry, 56n6
Bourne, George, 36–38, 42, 47
Breckinridge, Robert J., 55n6, 57,
71–73, 93, 95
Briggs, Charles A., 108n63
Brown, Guy Story, 40n22

Buddhism, 17
Bushnell, Horace, 47n45

Calhoun, John C., 40
calling, 115
Calvin, John, 26n18
on the Holy Spirit, 29, 124
on the second use of the law, 11
Canaan, 48
Carson, D. A., 7n7
Carter, Craig A., 7n7
Chan, Simon, 17n2
Chapell, Bryan, 115
chattel slavery, 51, 122, 124
Christ and culture, 7
Christendom, 8
Christianity, not merely a political
revolutionary movement, 122
Christian life, disciplines in, 17
Christian mysticism, 17n2
Christian nationalism, 9n13
Christian spirituality, 16–18
church
authority and prerogative of, 73
created and possessed by the Holy
Spirit, 124
engagement with the world, 125–27
as institute, 4–5
marginalization and irrelevance of, 25
mission of, 1

as organism, 4
politicization of, 21, 25, 69, 109,
    120
power of, xiii, 94
province of, 16, 26, 46, 53, 54,
    75–76, 98, 124
public voice of, 10
as a spiritual hospital, 124
spiritual independency of, 20
unity of, 41
See also spirituality of the church
church and state, 7, 53, 54
church polity, 20
civil religion, 123
Clay, Henry, 40n22, 45n39
coming age, 2–3
Communism, 114
Compromise of 1850, 43
confederacy, 55–56
Confederate States of America, 63
Constantine, 9
Cooper, Christopher C., 118n9
cotton industry, 35
Covenanters, 8, 46, 118

Dabney, Robert Lewis, 100n40, 101
Darwin, Charles, 5
Darwinism, and White supremacy,
    47n45
Davis, David Brion, 31n1
"Declaration and Testimony" (Presby-
    tery of Louisville), 88–98, 101
DeYoung, Kevin, 9n13, 19
doctrine, as basis of union, 107
Dred Scott decision (1857), 43

Engerman, Stanley L., 36n12
Erastianism, 95–96
Estelle, Bryan, 19, 28n23
Eusebius, 9
Evans, Christopher H., 5n3
extreme spirituality of the church, 22,
    109. *See also* "hyperspirituality" of
    the church

"faithful presence," 113n2
family, 26
Farmer, James O., Jr., 27n19
feudalism, 121n11
Floyd, George, 13n18
Fogel, Robert William, 36n12
Ford, Lacy K., 36n13
Foster, Richard, 17n2
founding fathers, on slavery, 40–41n24
French Revolution, 11
Freud, Sigmund, 5
Fugitive Slave Act, 43

Gardiner Spring Resolutions, 12, 60–66,
    85, 89, 92–93, 100n38, 109, 117
Garrison, William Lloyd, 33
General Assembly deliverances, 80–82
General Assembly of 1818, deliverance
    on slavery, 36–38, 41–43, 112, 124
General Assembly of 1861, 54, 58–66
General Assembly of 1862, 70–72, 102
General Assembly of 1863, 102
General Assembly of 1865, 76–85, 89
General Assembly of 1868, "Protest
    and Answer" to, 104–6
Gilbert, Greg, 19
Gladden, Washington, 5
gnosticism, 3
Goen, C. C., 69n6
good Samaritan, 4, 127
Goodwin, Doris Kearns, 123n15
gospel
    not about worldly success, 1
    spiritual message of, 2–3
governmental theory of the atonement,
    88n3, 104
Great Commission, 1, 3, 4
Gutjahr, Paul C., 87n1, 88n4, 99n36,
    101, 102n45

Ham/Canaan curse, 47–48
Harper, Kyle, 122n12
Harrill, J. Albert, 121n11
Hart, D. G., 18, 97n32

Wilberforce, William, 24
Willson, James Renwick, 8n11
Wilson, Douglas, 114n3
Wilson, Joseph Ruggles, 123
Wilson, Woodrow, 123

Wingard, Brian T., 21n14
"wokeness," 114
Wolfe, Stephen, 9n13
Wood, Gordon S., 35–36nn10–11
Wordsworth, William, 5n4

Scripture Index